T0291348

PARTNERSHIPS AND S CORPORATIONS

MISREPORTING INCOME AND TAX COMPLIANCE ISSUES

BUSINESS ISSUES, COMPETITION AND ENTREPRENEURSHIP

Additional books in this series can be found on Nova's website under the Series tab.

Additional e-books in this series can be found on Nova's website under the e-book tab.

BUSINESS ISSUES, COMPETITION AND ENTREPRENEURSHIP

PARTNERSHIPS AND
S CORPORATIONS

MISREPORTING INCOME
AND TAX COMPLIANCE ISSUES

KEITH PRESTON
EDITOR

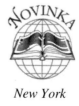

New York

Library of Congress Cataloging-in-Publication Data

ISBN: 978-1-63463-124-2

Published by Nova Science Publishers, Inc. † New York

CONTENTS

PREFACE

This book describes what is known about misreporting of flow-through income; assesses how much misreporting IRS identifies; and analyzes possible improvements in IRS's use of data to better identify partnerships and S corporations to consider examining. This book also analyzes individual tax return data to determine who earns pass-through business income and bears the burden of taxes on that income.

Chapter 1 - Since 1980, partnerships' and S corporations' share of business receipts increased greatly. These entities generally do not pay income taxes. Instead, income or losses (hundreds of billions of dollars annually) flow through to partners and shareholders to include on their income tax returns. GAO has previously reported that the misreporting of income by partners and shareholders poses a tax compliance risk.

GAO was asked to assess IRS's efforts to ensure compliance by partnerships and S corporations. This report (1) describes what is known about misreporting of flow-through income, (2) assesses how much misreporting IRS identifies, and (3) analyzes possible improvements in IRS's use of data to better identify partnerships and S corporations to consider examining. Comparing partnership, S corporation, and other entities' examination results, GAO analyzed 2003-2012 IRS data and evaluated possible improvement ideas stemming, in part, from prior GAO work, for how IRS identifies examination workload.

Chapter 2 - Pass-through businesses — sole proprietorships, partnerships, and S corporations — generate more than half of all business income in the United States. Pass-through income is, in general, taxed only once at the individual income tax rates when it is distributed to its owners. In contrast, the income of C corporations is taxed twice; once at the corporate level according to corporate tax rates, and then a second time at the individual tax rates when shareholders receive dividend payments or realize capital gains. This leads to the so-called ""double taxation"" of corporate profits.

This report analyzes individual tax return data to determine who earns pass-through business income and bears the burden of taxes on that income. The analysis finds that over 82% of net pass-through income is earned by taxpayers with an adjusted gross income (AGI) over $100,000, although these taxpayers account for just 23% of returns filed. A significant fraction of pass-through income is concentrated among upper-income earners. Taxpayers with AGI over $250,000, for example, receive 62% of pass-through income, but account for just over 6% of returns with pass-through income. A closer look at S corporations and partnerships shows passive income accounts for 10% and 25%, respectively, of their total income. This analysis, when combined with research on the corporate tax burden, suggests that higher-income taxpayers will generally bear most of the burden from increased pass-through taxes.

A number of proposed and scheduled tax changes would result in pass-throughs paying higher taxes. Several lawmakers and the Obama Administration, for example, have expressed interest in taxing large pass-throughs as corporations, which would subject some pass-throughs to an additional layer of taxation. Pass-through taxation could also increase if a tax reform that includes lower corporate tax rates that are paid for by the elimination or reduction of certain business tax benefits is enacted. Additionally, the scheduled expiration of the 2001/2003 tax cuts at the end of this year could increase taxes on pass-throughs by increasing individual tax rates. Lastly, a new 3.8% tax on passive income that was enacted as part of the Health Care and Education Reconciliation Act of 2010 (HCERA, P.L. 111-152) is set to take effect in 2013. The tax may apply to some pass-throughs.

While the analysis of these proposed and scheduled changes suggests that higher-income taxpayers will generally bear most of the burden from increased pass-through taxes, there are circumstances that could raise congressional concern. For example, an across-the-board expiration of the 2001/2003 individual tax rates will increase taxes for all pass-through owners. One option for preventing the tax burden from increasing for lower and middle class business owners is to allow the reduced rates to expire only for higher-income earners.

Concern has also risen over the new 3.8% tax on passive income and its effect on pass-throughs. The distributional analysis in this report shows, however, most S corporation and partnership income is the active type, and active business income is exempt from the 3.8% tax. The share of income that is passive, and potentially subject to the new tax, overwhelmingly accrues to higher-income taxpayers — 77% of passive partnership income and 93% of passive S corporation income went to taxpayers with AGI over $250,000. Sole proprietors could generally be expected to be exempt from the tax since most of their income is likely active.

In: Partnerships and S Corporations   ISBN: 978-1-63463-124-2
Editor: Keith Preston   © 2014 Nova Science Publishers, Inc.

Chapter 1

PARTNERSHIPS AND S CORPORATIONS: IRS NEEDS TO IMPROVE INFORMATION TO ADDRESS TAX NONCOMPLIANCE[*]

United States Government Accountability Office

WHY GAO DID THIS STUDY

Since 1980, partnerships' and S corporations' share of business receipts increased greatly. These entities generally do not pay income taxes. Instead, income or losses (hundreds of billions of dollars annually) flow through to partners and shareholders to include on their income tax returns. GAO has previously reported that the misreporting of income by partners and shareholders poses a tax compliance risk.

GAO was asked to assess IRS's efforts to ensure compliance by partnerships and S corporations. This report (1) describes what is known about misreporting of flow-through income, (2) assesses how much misreporting IRS identifies, and (3) analyzes possible improvements in IRS's use of data to better identify partnerships and S corporations to consider examining. Comparing partnership, S corporation, and other entities' examination results, GAO analyzed 2003-2012 IRS data and evaluated possible improvement ideas

---

[*] This is an edited, reformatted and augmented version of the United States Government Accountability Office publication, GAO-14-453, dated May 2014.

stemming, in part, from prior GAO work, for how IRS identifies examination workload.

WHAT GAO RECOMMENDS

GAO suggests that Congress consider requiring more partnerships and corporations to e-file their tax returns. GAO recommends, among other things, that IRS (1) develop a strategy to improve its information on the extent and nature of partnership misreporting, and (2) use the information to potentially improve how it selects partnership returns to examine. IRS stated it would consider all the recommendations and identify appropriate actions.

WHAT GAO FOUND

The full extent of partnership and S corporation income misreporting is unknown. The Internal Revenue Service's (IRS) last study of S corporations, using 2003-2004 data, estimated that these entities annually misreported about 15 percent (an average of $55 billion for 2003 and 2004) of their income. IRS does not have a similar study for partnerships. Using IRS data and the study results, GAO derived a rough-order-of-magnitude estimate of $91 billion per year of partnership and S corporation income being misreported by individuals for 2006 through 2009.

IRS examinations and automated document matching have not been effective at finding most of the estimated misreported income. For example, IRS reported that examinations identified about $16 billion per year of misreporting in 2011 and 2012, the bulk of which related to partnerships. However, such information about compliance results is not reliable. IRS estimated that 3 to 22 percent of the misreporting by partnerships was double counted due to some partnership income being allocated to other partnerships or related parties. Further, IRS does not know how income misreporting by partnerships affects taxes paid by partners. IRS does not have a strategy to improve the information. As a result, IRS does not have reliable information about its compliance results to fully inform decisions about allocating examination resources across different types of businesses.

IRS's processes for selecting returns to examine could be improved. Not all partnership and S corporation line items from paper returns are digitized, and IRS officials said that having more return information available electronically might improve examination selection. In 2011, about 65 percent of partnerships and S corporations electronically filed (e-filed). Certain large partnerships and S corporations are required by statute to e-file. Expanding the mandate would increase digitized data available for examination selection. Further, in 1995 GAO found that IRS's computer scoring system for selecting partnership returns to examine used outdated information. IRS does not have a strategy to update and use this information to select partnerships for examination. Relatively few partnerships are examined compared to other business entities, and many examinations result in no change in taxes owed. Improved examination selection based on more current information could generate more revenue and reduce IRS examinations of compliant taxpayers.

ABBREVIATIONS

AIMS	Audit Information Management System
AUR	Automated Underreporter
DIF	discriminant function
EOAD	Examination Operational Automation
IRS	Database Internal Revenue Service
LB&I	Large Business and International
NRP	National Research Program
RAS	Research, Analysis, and Statistics
SB/SE	Small Business/Self-Employed
SOI	Statistics of Income
TIGTA	Treasury Inspector General for Tax Administration

***

May 14, 2014

The Honorable Ron Wyden
Chairman
Committee on Finance
United States Senate

Dear Chairman Wyden:

Over the past few decades, partnerships and S corporations have accounted for an increasing share of business activity in the United States.[1] For example, from tax year 1980 to tax year 2008, these two types of business entities' share of all business receipts increased from about 7 percent to about 34 percent.[2]

Partnerships and S corporations are flow-through entities, which are entities that generally do not pay taxes themselves on income, but instead, pass income or losses to their partners and shareholders, who must include that income or loss on their income tax returns.[3] Each year, partnerships and S corporations allocate hundreds of billions of dollars of income to their partners and shareholders. Individuals, corporations, tax-exempt organizations, and other flow-through entities can be partners or shareholders and can receive allocations of flow-through income.[4]

Partnership and S corporation income may be misreported to the Internal Revenue Service (IRS) by both the partnerships and S corporations themselves, and the taxpayers to whom they allocate income.[5] For instance, in 2007, GAO reported that the tax gap—the difference between taxes owed and taxes paid on time—for income reported by individuals from partnerships, S corporations, estates, and trusts was $22 billion for 2001. Income from partnerships and S corporations was the primary driver for noncompliance for this area.[6] IRS's efforts to identify tax returns to examine for possible misreporting depend on data from both of these groups' returns. Resource limitations and interest in minimizing taxpayer burden prevent IRS from examining anything but a small fraction of the total number of tax returns—including from partnerships and S corporations—filed for a given tax year.

One challenge that IRS faces in ensuring that flow-through entities comply with tax reporting requirements is that these entities can be linked together in multitiered networks. For example, a partnership could be a partner in another partnership. In multitiered networks, flow-through entities receive allocations from other flow-through entities, and may pass the allocations through to still other flow-through entities on their way to taxpayers. While there are legitimate reasons for businesses to set up networks, such as isolating one part of a business from liability for the losses of another part, networks can also be used to evade taxes and make misreporting difficult for IRS to identify.[7]

You asked us to assess IRS's efforts to ensure compliance in reporting of partnership and S corporation income by individual taxpayers and by the entities themselves. The objectives of this report are to (1) describe what is known about the extent of income misreporting by partnerships and S corporations, and by the individuals to whom these entities allocate that income; (2) assess how much misreported partnership and S corporation income IRS identifies and assesses taxes on; and (3) analyze how IRS could improve its use of data to better identify partnerships and S corporations to consider for examination.

For the first two objectives, we collected and analyzed the latest available data from various IRS databases, which ranged from 2003 to 2012. Using these data, we reviewed IRS estimates of entity-level misreporting, estimated individuals' misreporting of income allocated by partnerships and S corporations, analyzed IRS's examination findings related to that income, and reviewed the amount of additional taxes that were assessed as a result of IRS's matching of individuals' tax returns against Schedule K-1 information reporting related to those returns, the only returns against which IRS routinely matched K-1s.[8] We also analyzed data that IRS provided on the extent and nature of tiering of partnerships and S corporations.

For the third objective, we reviewed various IRS documents and interviewed IRS officials to determine how IRS identifies partnership and S corporation returns for later classification and examination. In addition, we identified different approaches for improving how IRS identifies potentially noncompliant returns for eventual examination based on our audit findings as well as our past recommendations and recommendations made by the Treasury Inspector General for Tax Administration (TIGTA), and evaluated the approaches' costs and benefits.[9] We assessed whether the approaches could help IRS identify more noncompliance, make examinations more efficient, reduce taxpayer burden, or meet other IRS needs. For specific approaches, we evaluated whether they might reduce how often IRS examinations resulted in no changes to tax returns or how electronic filing (e-filing) rates for partnerships and S corporations compared to other e-filing rates.

We determined the reliability of the data we used through review of IRS's documentation describing the data, tests of internal consistency, tests for consistency with published IRS data, and interviews with IRS officials. We found the IRS databases we used to be reliable for the purposes of this report. All percentage estimates derived from samples used in this report have 95-percent confidence intervals that are within plus or minus 10 percentage points of the estimates themselves, unless otherwise specified. All other estimates in this report have 95-percent confidence intervals that are within plus or minus

10 percent of the estimates themselves, unless otherwise specified. Appendix I contains additional details about our scope and methodology.

We conducted this performance audit from January 2013 through May 2014 in accordance with generally accepted government auditing standards. Those standards require that we plan and perform the audit to obtain sufficient, appropriate evidence to provide a reasonable basis for our findings and conclusions based on our audit objectives. We believe that the evidence obtained provides a reasonable basis for our findings and conclusions based on our audit objectives.

BACKGROUND

Partnerships group two or more individuals or entities—such as corporations or other partnerships—to carry on a business. Individuals, corporations, trusts, estates, tax-exempt entities, and other partnerships may all be partners. S corporations may have between 1 and 100 shareholders. Individuals, certain trusts, estates, and certain tax-exempt entities may be S corporation shareholders.[10] Partnerships and S corporations must file tax returns (IRS Forms 1065 and 1120-S, respectively).

Partnerships and S corporations differ from C corporations—which are covered by subchapter C of the Internal Revenue Code and include nearly all publicly traded corporations—in that C corporations pay corporate income tax on their profits. Partnerships and S corporations do not directly pay taxes on the net income reported on Forms 1065 or 1120-S. Instead, they pass profits to partners and shareholders, respectively, who pay any applicable taxes.

In recent decades, partnership and S corporation activity has represented a growing share of business activity, while the share of C corporation activity has declined, as measured by gross business receipts, the revenue that a business receives from its trade or operations before subtracting expenses and deductions.[11] As a result, a larger share of business activity is now subject to taxation at the individual, rather than the corporate level, than in the past. According to IRS statistics compiled for tax year 1980 through tax year 2008, the percentage of business receipts taken in by partnerships and S corporations grew from about 7 percent to about 34 percent, as shown in figure 1.

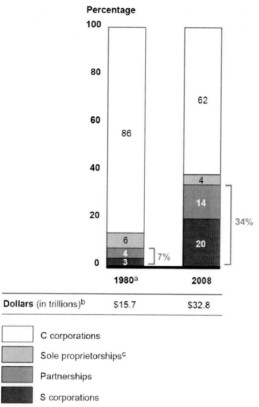

Source: GAO analysis of IRS data.
[a] The percentages for 1980 do not total 100 percent due to rounding.
[b] Dollar amounts are adjusted to calendar year 2013 dollars using the chain-weighted gross domestic product price index.
[c] A sole proprietorship is an unincorporated business that is owned by a single individual.

Figure 1. The Share of Gross Business Receipts by Partnerships and S Corporations Grew from about 7 Percent to about 34 Percent between Tax Year 1980 and Tax Year 2008.

There were about 4 million S corporations and 3 million partnerships in the United States in tax year 2008. However, the bulk of flow-through business activity was concentrated in a smaller number of entities. In the case of partnerships, 95 percent of business receipts in tax year 2008 went to the 260,000 partnerships with receipts of $1 million or more (see figure 2).

Partnerships and S corporations are required to send each of their partners and shareholders a Schedule K-1 that reports how much income or loss they allocated to that partner or shareholder in the past year, and to send a copy to IRS.[12] Individuals and business entities to which partnerships and S corporations allocated income are required to report that income on their income tax returns.

IRS has multiple compliance assurance processes. Two important ones for detecting misreporting of partnership and S corporation income are examinations (commonly known as audits) and K-1 matching.

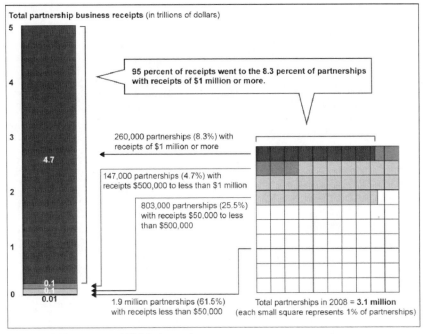

Source: GAO analysis of IRS information.

Note: Numbers may not match up precisely due to rounding.

Figure 2. Proportion of Aggregate Gross Partnership Business Receipts Earned by Partnerships of Different Sizes, Tax Year 2008.

Overview of Examinations and Examination Workload Identification

Examinations are IRS reviews of an entity's or individual's books and records conducted to verify what is reported on a tax return. They can be labor intensive and time consuming for IRS, but can detect complicated forms of noncompliance.

IRS may examine a flow-through entity, the partners or shareholders (such as individuals) who are allocated income from the flow-through, or—if the entity is part of tiered structure of related entities—IRS may examine the entire tiered network.

The examination process generally occurs in three steps. Typically, it starts with *return selection*—a largely automated process that selects tax returns for further review if they appear to be at risk for noncompliance. In the next step—*classification*—trained staff look at the selected tax returns and determine whether they warrant an examination, what issues should be examined, and how the examination should be conducted. In the final step— *examination*—a more detailed review of the return and other relevant information IRS possesses, such as information returns (for example, K-1s), is conducted. The examination generally includes contact with the taxpayer and a review of the taxpayer's books and records. It ends with a decision about whether to recommend no change, a refund, or additional tax assessment.

Overview of K-1 Matching

K-1 matching is a function of IRS's Automated Underreporter (AUR) program (see figure 3 for a description of the AUR process). AUR matches the information returns that IRS receives about a taxpayer with income reported on that taxpayer's Form 1040. Information returns are documents, such as W-2s (used to report wages) and K-1s, that third parties provide to taxpayers and IRS about taxpayers' income. K-1 matching aims to detect mismatches between each taxpayer's Form 1040 and K-1s, allowing IRS to detect taxpayers who misreport income from partnerships and S corporations. Because taxpayers know that IRS receives a copy of each K-1, matching encourages voluntary compliance at the taxpayer level.[13] K-1 matching of individual returns is not designed to detect misreporting about business operations at the flow-through entity level. Additionally, it does not match partnership and S corporation returns with the K-1s they receive from other flow-through entities.

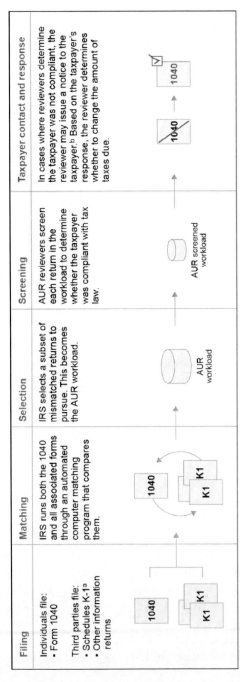

Filing	Matching	Selection	Screening	Taxpayer contact and response
Individuals file: • Form 1040 Third parties file: • Schedules K-1[a] • Other information returns	IRS runs both the 1040 and all associated forms through an automated computer matching program that compares them.	IRS selects a subset of mismatched returns to pursue. This becomes the AUR workload.	AUR reviewers screen each return in the workload to determine whether the taxpayer was compliant with tax law.	In cases where reviewers determine the taxpayer was not compliant, the reviewer may issue a notice to the taxpayer.[b] Based on the taxpayer's response, the reviewer determines whether to change the amount of taxes due.

Source: GAO analysis of IRS data.

[a] Schedules K-1 are information returns that partnerships and S corporations are required to send to each of their partners and shareholders, reporting how much income or loss they allocated to that partner or shareholder in the past year. They also send a copy to IRS.

[b] The reviewer will not issue a notice in cases where the reviewer does any of the following: determines that the discrepancy is below a certain dollar amount; transfers the case to another IRS unit or division, such as the examination function or Criminal Investigation; or adjusts the taxpayer's account without a notice, which is done when federal withholding or excess Social Security tax is the only issue.

Figure 3. IRS Automated Underreporter (AUR) Process.

DUE TO UNDETECTED MISREPORTING, INCOMPLETE COMPLIANCE DATA, AND DOUBLE COUNTING OF INCOME WITHIN NETWORKS, THE FULL EXTENT OF PARTNERSHIP AND S CORPORATION INCOME MISREPORTING IS UNKNOWN

There is substantial uncertainty surrounding the extent of income misreporting by partnerships and S corporations themselves, and by the individual taxpayers to whom the income is allocated.[14]

Partnerships and S Corporations

IRS has estimated misreporting by S corporations but not by partnerships. In IRS's most recent study of S corporation misreporting— covering tax years 2003 and 2004—IRS conducted detailed examinations of a sample of S corporation tax returns.[15] However, such a study inevitably cannot detect all misreporting. IRS analysis of the study did not include an adjustment for income that examiners were unable to detect, so the true amount of misreporting by S corporations may have been significantly larger than IRS reported, according to a preliminary report by an official from IRS's Office of Research, Analysis, and Statistics.[16] For those two years, using a weighted average, IRS estimated that S corporations misreported about $55 billion per year in net income.[17]

Because IRS has not conducted a similar study of partnerships since 1988, and does not have plans to conduct one, it does not have a similar estimate for partnerships. Moreover, estimating total partnership income or loss and the misreported amounts of income and loss is complicated by the fact that substantial portions of those amounts get double counted as they pass from one partnership to another.[18] IRS data show that in 2011, partnerships reported a total of $1,468 billion of income and $507 billion in losses.[19] About 31 percent of this income and 36 percent of the losses were allocated to other partnerships before ultimately being passed on to another party, resulting in double counting of this income and losses. Partnerships may also allocate income to others, including S corporations, estates, and trusts, which would complicate correcting for double counting. About 31 percent of partnerships were part of multitiered networks in tax year 2011, as shown in figure 4.[20] See appendix II for more information on tiering of flow-through networks.

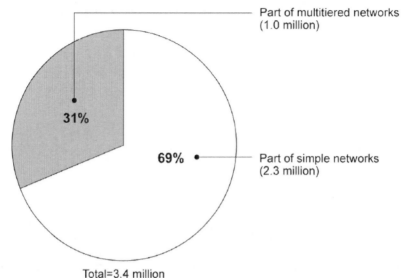

Total=3.4 million

Source: GAO analysis of IRS data.
Notes:

A simple network is a network that includes a flow-through entity that does not receive allocations from another flow-through entity nor allocate income to another flow-through entity. A multitiered network includes at least one flow-through entity that allocates income to another flow-through entity.

Because the database containing the data this figure is based on has incomplete data, the extent of tiering presented in this figure represents a minimum amount, and counts are approximate.

Numbers do not sum to total, and dividing entity counts by totals do not match up with percentages, due to rounding.

Figure 4. Tiering of Partnerships, Tax Year 2011.

Without a strategy for better estimating the extent and nature of partnership misreporting, IRS cannot make fully informed decisions on how to allocate resources across enforcement programs and across different types of business entities and taxpayers. IRS's strategic plan for 2009-2013 calls for IRS to develop improved research-driven methods and tools to detect and combat noncompliance and improve resource allocation. As we discussed in a 2012 report, optimizing resource allocation has the potential to bring in substantially more enforcement revenue.[21]

Individual Taxpayers

IRS's compliance research studies have produced data on flow-through income misreporting by individual taxpayers. Using this information, and considering various caveats and uncertainties, we estimated a rough order of magnitude of the misreporting to be $91 billion per year for tax years 2006 through 2009.[22]

This estimate does not cover all flow-through income. Only some types of income—ordinary business income, rental income, and guaranteed payments—can be included in an estimate of income that individuals misreported from partnerships and S corporations.[23] These items are reported on a section of the individual tax return specific to income from partnerships and S corporations. Some other types of income individuals receive via partnerships and S corporations, including interest, dividends, and royalties, cannot be estimated based on available data because they are combined with the same types of income from nonflow-through sources on another part of the individual tax return.[24]

Additionally, there is uncertainty surrounding any estimate of how much income individual taxpayers misreported due to presumed misreporting that IRS research examiners are inevitably unable to detect. IRS assumes that such misreporting exists and adjusts its estimates to account for it when it does its compliance studies on individual taxpayers. For individual taxpayers, an estimate of the rate of partnerships' and S corporations' misreporting of their own income can be incorporated into the adjustment, since errors at the entity level would generally be passed through to individual taxpayers. The individual misreporting rate would be expected to be at least as high as the misreporting rate for the entities that are allocating income to them. However, as mentioned above, IRS's most recent estimate of S corporation misreporting is itself uncertain, and IRS does not have a similar estimate for partnerships.

With these caveats in mind, we estimated, based on IRS research examination data, that in tax years 2006 through 2009, the annual average income that individual taxpayers were allocated from partnerships and S corporations was $517 billion, and annual average losses were $94 billion, for a net of $423 billion.[25] Of this $423 billion, we estimated that individual taxpayers misreported about $91 billion per year (this amount includes understated income plus overstated losses, less overstated income and understated losses). These taxpayers paid their taxes based on the misreported amounts, and we estimated that the $91 billion corresponded to about $19 billion per year in lost tax revenue. This $91 billion likely includes some of the

$55 billion of misreporting by S corporations, but IRS is unable to calculate how much.[26] Given all of the uncertainty involved, these estimates should both be considered rough orders of magnitude. See appendix III for details on our estimation methodology and more information on factors contributing to uncertainty, as well as a comparison of individual taxpayers' misreporting of income from partnerships and S corporations with misreporting of other types of income.

IRS Identified a Relatively Small Percentage of Estimated Misreported Income through Examinations and K-1 Matching and Lacks Reliable Information on Examination Results

Examinations

IRS examinations have not been effective at finding most of the misreported income discussed above. According to information that IRS collected for revenue agent examinations closed in fiscal years 2011 and 2012, IRS proposed increasing the total income reported by partnerships and S corporations by an annual average of about $16.3 billion.[27]

Additionally, for just partnerships, which accounted for the bulk of proposed partnership and S corporation adjustments, IRS estimated that from 3 percent to 22 percent of the proposed adjustments were double counted in the $16.3 billion total. An unknown amount of IRS's proposed adjustments to entity-level income included adjustments flowing through multiple tiers of flow-through entities or showing up in related returns, resulting in double counting. Thus, the true amount of unique adjustments might be smaller than IRS's records seem to show.

Adjustments at the entity level can generally only result in increased taxes to the extent that adjustments and assessments are subsequently made at the partner or shareholder level. IRS officials said that because of computer systems limitations, they did not have an estimate of the extent to which proposed adjustments to income at the entity level increased actual taxes collected at the partner or shareholder level. Because IRS does not know how much of what it proposes in adjustments for partnerships relates to non-duplicate income, nor to what extent those adjustments result in increased taxes collected, it cannot know its return on investment for partnership examinations. IRS's examination rate for partnerships is much lower than the rate for C corporations and for sole proprietorships. Without a strategy for estimating the effectiveness of partnership examinations, IRS cannot know whether the differences in examination rates across different types of business entities are justified, i.e., whether it is optimally allocating its enforcement resources across its enforcement programs. As mentioned above, IRS's strategic plan calls for IRS to develop improved research-driven methods and tools to detect and combat noncompliance and improve resource allocation, and optimizing resource allocation has the potential to bring in substantially more enforcement revenue. However, identifying the taxes collected that result from proposed adjustments at the partnership level would require IRS to upgrade its computer systems, which would require funding.

As the data in table 1 indicate, partnerships differ significantly in terms of the types of income that they earn through their own activities or receive from other partnerships, estates, or trusts. These differing characteristics may indicate that separate enforcement approaches, focusing on different compliance issues, are appropriate for each subpopulation. One significant distinction among partnerships is whether they generate ordinary business income of their own. More than 40 percent of partnerships have no ordinary business income or loss, and about 20 percent of the ordinary business income and losses that partnerships report is simply passed on from other partnerships. A large portion of partnership income other than ordinary business income is portfolio income. Partnerships can receive interest, dividend, or royalty payments directly from the original issuers of these payments, or they can receive them as pass-through amounts from other partnerships. Rental income (primarily from real estate) is another important type of income.

IRS examination program monitoring tabulations currently do not track examination rates, no-change rates, or enforcement revenue to cost ratios for partnership subpopulations, defined in terms of the types of income they earn. Consequently, we do not know whether these measures differ significantly across the various groups. Without a strategy for better estimating the extent and nature of misreporting by different subpopulations of partnerships, and the effectiveness of partnership examinations in detecting misreporting by different subpopulations of partnerships, IRS cannot enhance its case selection processes to focus its enforcement tools on activities that pose the highest risk of noncompliance, as is called for in its strategic plan.

For IRS to make informed decisions in expanding its flow-through income compliance initiatives, it would have to resolve what it considers to be high-priority problems with the accuracy, completeness, and timeliness of K-1 data.

In July 2013, an IRS data issues team found that these issues included K-1s that were at times missing, unable to be matched to partnership returns or validated, unavailable for months, subject to misreporting by recipients, and only partially allocating partnership income. The IRS team believed the problems hurt IRS's ability to identify partner, partnership, and network compliance issues and use risk assessment tools to evaluate them.

To resolve these K-1 data issues, IRS staff presented to IRS management 15 short- and long-term potential solutions, most of which IRS is waiting to address because of funding considerations. The solutions included what IRS considered to be critical fixes needed in 2 to 3 years, but IRS needed more analysis to identify and address partnership return data issues. Without approving other solutions, management approved costing out three 1-to-2-year fixes, including testing K-1 data programming errors and checking that the data were correctly processed. Once the costing out was completed, management expected to decide whether to fund these three fixes, although it did not provide us a date for making that decision. It had approved nothing else.

For individual taxpayers, in examinations closed in fiscal years 2011 and 2012, IRS proposed adjusting the total income allocated to the individuals from partnerships and S corporations by an annual average of about $2.9 billion.[28] We calculated this amount based on data from IRS's Examination Operational Automation Database on examinations of taxpayers' returns. Only some types of income from partnerships and S corporations—such as ordinary business income and rental income— could be included in this amount. Other types, including interest, dividends, and royalties, could not be included because as noted earlier, they are combined with the same types of income from nonflow-through sources on individual taxpayers' returns. Based on an estimated tax rate range of 15 percent to 35 percent, the adjustments to income would have corresponded to between $450 million and $1 billion in taxes assessed.[29]

Some of these $2.9 billion in adjustments potentially would have been made due to the $16 billion in adjustments at the partnership and S corporation level, but as mentioned above, IRS officials told us that they could not quantify the extent to which this would have been the case.

Table 1. Flow-through Amounts for Partnership Income and Deductions, by Type, Tax Year 2011

Selected aggregate data from tax year 2011 partnership returns	Percent of partnerships reporting this item	Aggregate net positive income (billions)	Aggregate net losses or deductions (billions)	Absolute value of amounts received from other nontaxable entities as a percent of the total absolute value for the line item[a]
Ordinary business income (loss)	58.4%	$528.0	$272.3	20.4%
Portfolio income (interest, dividends, and royalties)	31.2	314.5	–	Not identifiable
Net rental real estate income (loss)	43.1	102.6	94.4	27.9
Other net rental income (loss)	2.0	7.2 (+/-14%)	5.1 (+/-13%)	Not identifiable
Capital gain (loss)	14.4	599.5	157.3	32.7
Other income (loss)	5.2	227.6	46.5	Not identifiable
Guaranteed payments to partners	9.5	63.5	–	Not applicable
Schedule K deductions	27.7	–	290.9	Not identifiable
Total net positive income (loss) allocated to partners[b]		**$1,467.7**	**$506.9**	**32.0**

Source: GAO analysis of IRS data.

Notes

Percent errors are used for dollar estimates. Results with relative margins of error greater than plus or minus 30 percent are omitted, and relative margins of error greater than plus or minus 10 percent are listed in parentheses. All other dollar estimates are within plus or minus 10 percent of the reported values. Percentage point errors are used for percentage estimates, and all percentage estimates are within plus or minus 10 percentage points of the reported values.

[a] For the last row the numerator equals amounts received from other partnerships based on the Analysis of Net Income (Loss) section of Schedule K of Form 1065. For the other rows the numerators equal amounts received from other partnerships, estates, and trusts.

[b] Rows do not sum to total net positive income (loss) allocated to partners because there is netting of different types of income for each taxpayer (a taxpayer may have positive business income offset by a capital loss) and the deductions are netted from income rather than added as a negative amount to the loss column.

K-1 Matching

As previously noted, IRS matches K-1s to individual tax returns, but IRS does not routinely match K-1s or other information returns to partnership and S corporation tax returns. Matching K-1s to partnership and S corporation tax returns might provide another tool for detecting noncompliance by these types of entities. IRS's strategic plan calls for IRS to develop improved research-driven methods and tools to detect and combat noncompliance and improve resource allocation, improve compliance by leveraging third-party reporting information, and streamline processes to increase the timeliness of enforcement. Rather than waiting until costing of data fixes is completed for further management involvement, management could begin planning now for how to use the improved data. Specifically, IRS could develop a plan for testing, or otherwise analyzing the data, to, for instance, determine whether matching at the entity level of some combination of K-1s and other information returns, could assist in verifying compliance. Matching might assist directly, by detecting misreported income, or indirectly by helping identify returns with examination potential. Without such a plan, when the costing of the data fixes is completed IRS will know the costs but perhaps not all of the benefits of moving to implement the data fixes.

For individual taxpayers, because of the way IRS tracks tax assessments through AUR, only a portion of the net assessments that resulted from K-1 matching can be definitively determined.[30] Specifically, when there are mismatches for both K-1 income and other types of income, IRS's AUR data systems do not separate out the K-1 amounts. With this caveat in mind, K-1 matching definitively resulted in net tax assessments of $24 million for tax year 2009, the latest year for which complete data were available. The actual amount could be higher, but is probably a relatively small portion of the $19 billion of unpaid taxes we estimated individuals misreported of partnership and S corporation income. The entire AUR program assessed $8 billion for more than 50 different categories of income and expenses.

K-1 matching through AUR, as noted above, is not used to detect misreporting between entities in a tiered network, nor is it designed to detect ordinary business income misreported on a K-1. As a consequence, the information on K-1s may match what is on individuals' 1040s, but both documents may understate the true income amount. More details about K-1 matching are discussed in appendix IV.

OPTIONS FOR IRS TO IMPROVE IDENTIFICATION OF PARTNERSHIPS AND S CORPORATIONS TO CONSIDER EXAMINING INVOLVE CHALLENGES, SOME OF WHICH COULD BE MITIGATED

There are various means through which IRS could improve how it selects partnership and S corporation tax returns to examine. As we have concluded previously, improving examination selection could have two positive impacts: increasing enforcement revenue by better focusing examinations on noncompliant taxpayers and reducing burden by reducing unnecessary audits of compliant taxpayers.[31]

IRS must decide how to allocate its enforcement resources based on limited information. IRS typically examines about 0.4 percent to 0.5 percent of partnership and S corporation returns per year, compared to about 1.4 percent to about 1.6 percent of C corporations, and 1.5 to 1.9 percent of nonfarm sole proprietorships that did not claim the earned income tax credit. Figure 5 shows these rates for fiscal year 2012.

The results of partnership and S corporation examinations are difficult to interpret. On one hand, IRS's rate for not recommending adjustments to income or expense items on partnership and S corporation examinations is relatively high. In fiscal years 2010 through 2012, no-change rates ranged between 42 percent and 46 percent for partnerships and 34 percent and 39 percent for S corporations. These rates are computed for the business entity. They do not reflect adjustments at the entity level that did not result in adjustments to the ultimate partners' or shareholders' individual returns.[32] No-change rates for partnerships and S corporations exceeded those for nonfarm sole proprietorships and C corporations in all 3 fiscal years from 2010 through 2012.

Table 2. Average Proposed IRS Adjustment to Income for Partnership and S Corporation Revenue Agent Examinations, Fiscal Year 2012

IRS division	Proposed adjustment per tax return	
	Partnerships[a]	S corporations
Small Business/Self-Employed	$126,867	$90,409
Large Business and International	$5,292,472	$484,751

Source: GAO analysis of IRS data.

Note: We focused on revenue agent examinations of partnerships and S corporations because tax compliance officers conduct very few examinations of these entities. In general, revenue agents conduct examinations of more complex tax returns, including partnerships and corporations, while tax compliance officers primarily conduct examinations of individual taxpayers.

[a] IRS may double count some proposed adjustments to income in partnership examinations due to income flowing through multitiered networks and appearing in related returns.

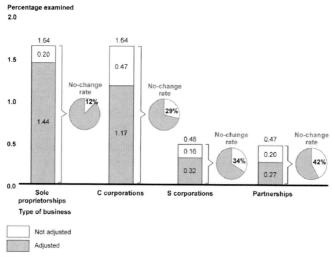

Source: IRS.

Figure 5. Fiscal Year 2012 Examination and Adjustment Rates for Different Types of Tax Returns.

On the other hand, when IRS revenue agents proposed income adjustments after partnership and S corporation examinations, the dollars were significant in absolute size, as shown in table 2. As may be expected given the size of the entities involved, the average proposed income adjustments for IRS's Large Business and International (LB&I) division returns were higher than for its Small Business/Self-Employed (SB/SE) division returns. However, as was the case with no-change rates, the proposed adjustments at the entity level do not necessarily show whether the ultimate partners or shareholders paid any additional tax at the individual level.

More Tax Return Digitization May Improve Workload Identification, but Digitizing All Partnership and S Corporation Return Items Is Not an Immediate IRS Priority

Not all partnership and S corporation line items are digitized. IRS officials said that having more return information available electronically might improve examination selection. For instance, when IRS subject matter experts with examination experience suggested filters for an SB/SE research project to use to identify potentially noncompliant preparers of partnership and S corporation returns, the lack of transcription prevented SB/SE from using all of the filters.[33]

Enhancing digitization of paper-filed partnership and S corporation returns would involve costs to IRS. In 2010, the direct labor costs and related overhead to transcribe all then-nontranscribed lines on partnership and S corporation returns would have exceeded $6 million for SB/SE and LB&I. This amount did not include significant direct labor costs for other processing functions such as input correction or quality review or costs to reprogram submission processing or post-processing systems, according to IRS officials. Responding to our recommendation from 2011, IRS considered studying the benefits of transcribing items from many forms to match against already-calculated costs.[34] However, according to an official in IRS's Return Preparer Office in September 2013, it decided against the study because of resource needs and budget constraints. By not transcribing more partnership and S corporation line items, IRS might be forgoing proposed adjustments to income that could result in increased tax assessments that might offset the cost of added transcription. However, according to an IRS official, more transcription might not be IRS's highest-priority partnership data problem. A higher-priority problem would be the issues described earlier with the accuracy, completeness, and timeliness of K-1 data. Within that context, IRS considered improving transcription a critical fix needed in 2 to 3 years. By that time, about 5 years would have passed since our 2011 recommendation, which we continue to believe has merit, but resource issues could still exist.

Increasing Electronic Filing Would Increase Digitization, and the Added Burden on Taxpayers Could Be Mitigated

Increasing electronic filing (e-filing) of partnership and S corporation tax returns would increase the amount of tax return data that arrive at IRS already digitized. Increasing the amount of digitized information arriving at IRS would reduce IRS processing costs and also reduce the cost of transcribing information from the remaining paper returns. One way to increase e-filing is for Congress to mandate it.

Currently, partnerships with more than 100 partners are required by law to e-file. Corporations, including S corporations, must e-file if they have assets of $10 million or more and file at least 250 returns during a calendar year.[35] However, under current law, e-filing cannot be required for partnerships with 100 partners or less or corporations, including S corporations, unless the entity is required to file at least 250 returns during a calendar year.[36]

The percentages of partnerships and S corporations that e-file tax returns have been growing rapidly in recent years, reaching 64 percent and 66 percent, respectively, in tax year 2011, the latest year for which data are available. IRS has projected rapid continued growth for the next couple of years and a leveling off after that, meaning that some paper-filed returns will always be expected.[37] However, as noted before, IRS will not be able to transcribe more partnership and S corporation line items off the remaining paper-filed returns, at least in the short term.

Unless all returns are digitized, IRS will not be able to use all return line items in its examination selection process. Less than full digitization limits IRS in selecting the most productive returns to examine and increases the likelihood of it examining compliant taxpayers. As noted above, transcribing the remaining paper returns is not a priority. Without a low-cost way to digitize paper returns, digitizing them is at risk of remaining an unfunded critical fix.

There are various forms a partnership and S corporate e-file mandate could take, including:

- requiring paid tax return preparers to e-file partnership and corporate returns they prepare;
- requiring e-filing based on a different number of partners in a partnership than is the case now;
- requiring e-filing based on whether a partnership already has a special responsibility and requirement to file a balance sheet anyway and, therefore, may more easily adapt to a new requirement than others can; and
- requiring e-filing based on the size of a partnership's or corporation's assets, with different asset requirements than now exist.[38]

Any option for an e-filing mandate would impose some burden on tax return filers. However, the extent of the burden may be small, since about 90 percent of partnerships and S corporations already use a paid preparer. Additionally, any burden could be mitigated. Waivers allowing paper filing in hardship and other special cases could eliminate burden for some tax return filers, and thresholds limiting the requirement to entities of a certain size (based on number of partners or some other measure) would eliminate the burden for entities below that size. Also, phase-in periods could allow time for entities to adjust. When IRS implemented the preparer e-file mandate for individuals, it found that the number of hardship waivers was fewer than anticipated, about 2,250 versus the 6,000 that had been expected.

IRS's Computer Scoring System for Identifying Partnership Returns to Examine Uses Outdated Formulas, but Upgrading Faces Challenges

SB/SE's partnership discriminant function (DIF) model to identify entities to examine was built on data that are now outdated, and does not capture partnership compliance issues related to tiering.[39] We pointed out in 1995 that because the formulas the model relied on were developed using data from the 1980s and tax laws and taxpayer behaviors had changed, the model unreliably indicated partnership compliance.[40] At the time, IRS said that it was planning to develop new formulas in 1998. However, SB/SE is still using the same DIF formulas.

Despite the model's formulas being outdated, indications are mixed on whether the partnership DIF model needs upgrading or is adequately identifying a productive workload of potentially noncompliant returns compared to other workload identification methods. In two 2012 reports, TIGTA found that no-change rates for partnership and S corporation returns selected by the DIF model and examined by nontrainee SB/SE revenue agents greatly exceeded those for other SB/SE partnership and S corporation returns examined by nontrainees.[41] On the other hand, when training examinations are included, LB&I, which did not use the DIF model, often had a higher no-change rate for revenue agent examinations for partnerships and S corporations than SB/SE, which used the DIF model. LB&I pointed out that its blend of returns to be examined may differ from SB/SE's, skewing the comparison.

According to IRS officials, updating the partnership DIF model could be complicated, expensive, and time consuming, taking resources from possibly productive examinations and having an unknown outcome. However, without determining whether an improved partnership DIF model should be developed after IRS has better information on noncompliance and program effectiveness, IRS cannot know whether it is missing an opportunity to select partnership returns for examination more effectively. IRS's strategic plan calls for IRS to develop improved research-driven methods and tools to improve resource allocation and to enhance its case-selection processes in order to focus its enforcement tools on activities that pose the highest risk of noncompliance. IRS officials told us they have started to look into ways to develop a new partnership DIF model, but there is no strategy, time frame, or plan for completing this effort.

IRS Is Beginning to Follow up Its Work on Filters to Be Used in Examination

In 1995 we identified filters, that is, flags that detect certain characteristics of partnerships whose examinations were the most productive for IRS to examine. In 2012, TIGTA did the same thing for both partnerships and S corporations.[42] For instance, for returns selected by the DIF model and for returns related to them, TIGTA found the examinations of real estate or construction partnerships with two partners and a reported loss were highly productive in terms of the size of recommended adjustments. Similar to what we had suggested more than a decade earlier, TIGTA recommended that, as resources become available, SB/SE analyze partnership and S corporation data files looking for ways to better identify productive returns for audit.

In response, in 2013, SB/SE researchers expanded an earlier study of partnership and S corporation returns to test the efficacy for examination selection of some new automated filters. They tested the filters on completed examinations to determine if using the filters could have resulted in a lower no-change rate. Three of the filters that were tested showed some promise in terms of reduced no-change rates. The researchers recommended that the SB/SE examination function use the promising filters to screen returns that the DIF model selected for examination and validate that the filters reduce the no-change rate below historical averages and are operationally feasible. According to SB/SE officials, they have begun that process.

CONCLUSION

Partnerships and S corporations account for billions of dollars of unpaid taxes and their share of business activity is growing. This underscores the importance of understanding the effectiveness of IRS's partnership and S corporation tax law enforcement efforts.

Currently, IRS examines a small fraction of partnership and S corporation tax returns. Other forms of businesses, such as C corporations and sole proprietorships, are examined at rates that are several times higher. IRS cannot make fully informed decisions about whether this allocation of enforcement resources is justified because it has limited information about the extent and nature of income misreporting by partnerships and S corporations as well as about the effectiveness of its examinations at detecting such misreporting. This also leaves IRS unable to make a fully informed, data-based decision about whether or not to update one of its major partnership examination selection tools, the DIF formula.

We identified two additional opportunities to better use data to improve compliance by flow-through entities. First, enabling greater digitization of tax return information would help IRS identify which partnership and S corporation tax returns would be most productive to examine. In the absence of funding for transcription, one way to increase digitization is a statutory mandate requiring increased e-filing of partnership and S corporation tax returns. Improving IRS's selection of partnership and S corporation returns to examine would also benefit compliant taxpayers whose returns may otherwise be selected for examination. Further, expanded e-filing would reduce IRS's tax return processing costs.

Second, IRS may be able to take advantage of its ongoing efforts to improve the quality of K-1 data to test whether compliance processes could be improved. Issues with the accuracy and timely availability of K-1 data have been a concern to IRS. Planning now for how to use the improved data would leave IRS well positioned to analyze options for improving its partnership and S corporation compliance programs.

MATTER FOR CONGRESSIONAL CONSIDERATION

Congress should consider expanding the mandate for partnerships and corporations to electronically file their tax returns to cover a greater share of filed returns.

RECOMMENDATIONS FOR EXECUTIVE ACTION

We recommend that the Commissioner of Internal Revenue take the following steps:

- Develop and implement a strategy to better estimate
  (1) the extent and nature of partnership misreporting, and
  (2) the effectiveness of partnership examinations in detecting this misreporting.
- Use the better information on noncompliance and program effectiveness to determine
  (1) whether the differences in examination rates across different types of business entities are justified, and
  (2) whether an improved tool for selecting partnerships for examination, such as an updated partnership DIF, should be developed.
- While IRS works to improve the quality of its Schedule K-1 data, develop a plan for conducting testing or other analysis to determine whether the improved Schedule K-1 data, perhaps combined with other IRS information about businesses and taxpayers, could be used more effectively to ensure compliance with the reporting of flow-through income.

AGENCY COMMENTS AND OUR EVALUATION

We sent a draft of this report to the Commissioner of Internal Revenue for comment. We received written comments from IRS's Deputy Commissioner for Services and Enforcement on May 6, 2014. We also received technical comments from IRS, which we incorporated into the final report where appropriate.

In its written comments, IRS said that it had not yet fully evaluated GAO's recommendations but expressed concerns regarding actions requiring a significant expenditure of resources. However, it said it would consider all of GAO's recommendations and identify appropriate IRS actions while keeping resource limitations in mind. It is these very resource limitations—which we recognize in this report—that underscore the importance of our recommendations to develop better information for making decisions on how to allocate existing resources.

Sincerely yours,

James R. White
Director, Tax Issues
Strategic Issues Team

APPENDIX I. OBJECTIVES, SCOPE, AND METHODOLOGY

The objectives of this report are to (1) describe what is known about the extent of income misreporting by partnerships and S corporations, and by the individuals to whom these entities allocate that income; (2) assess how much misreported partnership and S corporation income IRS identifies and assesses taxes on; and (3) analyze how IRS could improve its use of data to better identify partnerships and S corporations to consider for examination.

To describe what is known about the extent of income misreporting by partnerships and S corporations, we reviewed what IRS's National Research Program (NRP) had done at the entity level. For NRP, IRS selects a random sample of tax returns to examine and strives to verify information taxpayers and others reported or should have reported. We reviewed NRP documents and information on the 2003-04 entity-level study of S corporations, which was IRS's most recent study of S corporations. We also interviewed NRP officials about that study and what information was available about partnerships.

To describe what is known about the extent of income misreporting by individuals with income from partnerships and S corporations, we obtained data from NRP for tax years 2006 through 2009, the most recent years for which data were available. At the individual level, IRS conducts NRP studies annually. IRS uses the NRP data to estimate the tax gap and update return selection formulas used in planning examinations. Using these data, we estimated the amount of individual taxpayers' misreporting of income and losses from partnerships and S corporations on their Forms 1040, *U.S. Individual Income Tax Return*. We adjusted our raw result based on an IRS estimate of net misreporting percentage. See appendix III for a discussion of our and IRS's estimation techniques. For this analysis, we looked only at partnership and S corporation income that was separately reported on Schedule E (Form 1040), *Supplemental Income and Loss*. Some income from partnerships and S corporations may also be included within, and reported under, other line items on Form 1040, such as capital gains.

To calculate the amount of taxes that corresponded to our misreporting estimate, we used NRP data to calculate the income and misreporting that related to individuals with different effective tax rates (defined as total tax divided by adjusted gross income). Looking at taxpayers with effective tax rates between 15 percent and 35 percent, we calculated lower and upper bounds for the amount of tax that would have been owed on their misreported income from partnerships and S corporations.[43]

To assess how much misreported partnership and S corporation income IRS identifies and assesses taxes on, we obtained data from IRS's Audit Information Management System (AIMS), Examination Operational Automation Database (EOAD), and Automated Underreporter (AUR) program on K-1 matching. From AIMS, we obtained data on IRS proposed adjustments to partnership and S corporation tax returns for fiscal years 2011 and 2012, the latest years for which information was available when we obtained it.

From EOAD, we obtained data on IRS proposed adjustments to individual tax returns for fiscal years 2011 and 2012, the most recent years for which complete data were available. With these data, we calculated proposed adjustments to income and losses from partnerships and S corporations, to income and losses from estates and trusts, and to short-and long-term gains and losses from partnerships, S corporations, estates, and trusts. Based on the proposed adjustments and estimated tax brackets, we estimated the amount of taxes assessed based on these examinations.

Using AUR data for tax year 2009, the most recent year for which complete data were available, we reviewed the minimum amount of taxes assessed through matching K-1s against individual tax returns, the only returns against which IRS routinely matched K-1s. The minimum amount was based on returns for which K-1 discrepancies were the only matching discrepancies. We also determined the total amount of assessments that were not attributed to specific types of income, an unknown portion of which might be due to K-1 matching.

We interviewed officials from IRS's examination and AUR programs to determine the reliability of the data and to discuss examination and AUR operations. For contextual purposes, we analyzed IRS Statistics of Income (SOI) partnership data for 2011. Specifically, we determined income, losses, and percentages of income received from other partnerships, estates, or trusts for partnerships earning different kinds of income.

To analyze how IRS could improve its use of data to better identify partnerships and S corporations to consider for examination, we analyzed examination statistics derived from AIMS. For example, to see whether IRS's identification of potential examinations differed across different kinds of entities, we compared the percentage of partnership and S corporation returns that IRS examined to the percentage of C corporation and sole proprietorship returns that it examined. We also compared the rate at which IRS examinations recommended no adjustments to items reported on partnership and S corporation returns to no-change rates for examinations of C corporations and sole proprietorships.

We reviewed IRS guidance and interviewed IRS officials to learn how IRS identifies partnership and S corporation returns for later classification and examination and to understand to what extent the process is automated. From various documents, including GAO and Treasury Inspector General for Tax Administration (TIGTA) reports and recommendations, and interviews with IRS and Treasury officials, we evaluated the costs and benefits of various approaches we encountered that could improve IRS's use of data to better identify partnerships and S corporations to consider for examination and reduce the no-change rate for partnership and S corporation examinations.[44] We assessed whether the approaches included steps that IRS was taking or possibly could take to identify more noncompliance, make examinations more efficient, reduce taxpayer burden, or meet other IRS needs. More specifically, the approaches covered the following:

- **Increasing K-1 and partnership and S corporation return transcription and other digitization.** While considering this approach, we determined—from IRS transcription guidance and from interviews with IRS officials—how much of the data filed on paper K-1s and partnership and S corporation returns are not digitized into IRS databases. We also determined any resulting ramifications for workload identification. From IRS documentation and officials, we determined the details of how IRS plans to fix problems with the timeliness, completeness, and accuracy of K-1s to better use the information for workload identification.

- **Increasing partnership and S corporation return electronic filing.** We reviewed documents and interviewed IRS and Department of the Treasury officials about e-filing. More specifically, we explored the status of 2003 TIGTA ideas and subsequent legislative proposals on mandating more e-filing of partnership returns. As part of this effort, we reviewed past and projected e-filing rates prepared by IRS's Office of Research, Analysis, and Statistics (RAS), including SOI, and determined how many partnerships and S corporations would be affected by various enhancements to the e-filing mandate. We also compared e-filing rates for partnerships and S corporations to other e-filing rates.

- **Upgrading the computer scoring system for identifying partnership returns to eventually examine.** From various IRS and other documents and officials, we reviewed the history of IRS's computer scoring system, known as the discriminant function, or DIF, and the challenges to changing the system. We also reviewed TIGTA reports relating to the system.

- **Analyzing partnership and S corporation data files to identify workload.** In accordance with 2012 TIGTA and 1995 GAO ideas on using IRS databases, we obtained documentation regarding IRS efforts to use partnership and S corporation databases to develop examination leads and to select returns to examine.

In addition to our main objectives, we also provided the following information in the appendixes. For appendix II, to describe the extent and nature of multitiered networks of partnerships and S corporations, we obtained data from RAS on the tiering characteristics of partnerships and S corporations. The data related to a particular entity include information for all owners of at least 0.1 percent of that entity. Using data for tax year 2011, the most recent year for which complete and reliable data were available in the K-1 database that RAS used, we developed charts describing the relevant information. We interviewed RAS officials to determine the reliability of the data.

For appendix III, to compare individual taxpayers' misreporting of income from partnerships and S corporations with other income types, we calculated:

- net misreporting amounts;
- the percentage of taxpayers who misreported;

- the median amount of misreporting; and
- the net misreporting percentage for the following categories of income: (1) income from partnerships and S corporations, (2) other business income subcategories reported on Schedule E of Form 1040, and business income categories on Form 1040 itself, with estimated reported incomes with absolute values greater than $10 billion, and (3) the six nonbusiness income categories with estimated reported incomes of more than $150 billion reported on Form 1040.

We determined confidence intervals for all our estimates. Although we adjusted our estimate of misreporting of income from partnerships and S corporations based on an IRS estimate of net misreporting percentage, as mentioned above, we presented both the adjusted and unadjusted estimates in appendix III since we did not make comparable adjustments for the other income categories. We also compared the results for each income category with reported IRS determinations of whether the category was subject to little or no third-party information reporting, some information reporting, or substantial information reporting that IRS could match against Form 1040 reporting. We interviewed officials from RAS to determine the reliability of the NRP data and to discuss the adjustments that IRS makes to the data to calculate its reported net misreporting percentage and tax gap estimates.

For appendix IV, we calculated and compared the no-change rates in the AUR workload for K-1 matching and for all matching. We also attended and asked questions at a joint Information Reporting Program Advisory Committee and Internal Revenue Service Advisory Council meeting to obtain views on K-1 matching from paid tax return preparers and other relevant stakeholders.

We tested the reliability of NRP, AUR, EOAD, AIMS, and SOI data for previous GAO engagements, and we supplemented our knowledge through interviews with IRS officials and through documentation review, and, where applicable, electronic checks. We also tested these data for internal consistency, and for consistency with other IRS data when available. For example, for AIMS data we analyzed, we tested numbers against information published in TIGTA reports and IRS's Data Book, which annually provides information on returns filed, taxes collected, enforcement, taxpayer assistance, the IRS budget and workforce, and other selected activities. We also checked that the data extracts we used from different parts of RAS, including SOI, were consistent with each other and with information from the IRS Oversight Board. All percentage estimates derived from samples used in this report have

95-percent confidence intervals that are within plus or minus 10 percentage points of the estimates themselves, unless otherwise specified. All other estimates in this report have 95-percent confidence intervals that are within plus or minus 10 percent of the estimates themselves, unless otherwise specified.

We tested the K-1 data that IRS provided for internal consistency and consistency with published IRS data, verified the programming IRS used to create tables summarizing the K-1 data, and interviewed the IRS official who created the tables. Based on IRS documents and interviews with IRS officials, data in the K-1 database may be incomplete. Some K-1s may be missing from the database because of problems such as partnerships and S corporations failing to file K-1s, IRS errors, and timing problems. However, given IRS's estimates of the level of incompleteness, we believe that any inaccuracies would not change percentage results enough to change the overall conclusions presented in this report. In general, the amounts of tiering shown represent minimums and entity counts are approximate because the missing data would add more entities and linkages to the tables and charts we present.

We found the IRS databases we used to be reliable for the purposes of this report. We conducted this performance audit from January 2013 through May 2014 in accordance with generally accepted government auditing standards. Those standards require that we plan and perform the audit to obtain sufficient, appropriate evidence to provide a reasonable basis for our findings and conclusions based on our audit objectives. We believe that the evidence obtained provides a reasonable basis for our findings and conclusions based on our audit objectives.

APPENDIX II. MULTITIERED NETWORKS OF PARTNERSHIPS AND S CORPORATIONS

Many flow-through entities are connected to each other in tiered networks. As we have reported before, networks of related entities are a feature of modern business organizations.[45] Many legitimate reasons explain why business owners may choose to use a network of related entities to conduct operations. For example, networks can be used to isolate one line of business from the potential liabilities or risk of business loss of another, to manage a business's financing arrangements, or to separate ventures based in different states and countries. However, networks can also be used in complex tax evasion schemes that are difficult for IRS to identify. More complex networks also make businesses more difficult for IRS to examine. IRS officials said that some businesses may believe that if their networks are sufficiently complex, they will be difficult for IRS to examine. Therefore, it is helpful to understand the extent to which partnerships and S corporations are involved in multitiered networks, as well as the complexity of such networks. See the text box for tiering terminology. Many of the above concepts are illustrated in figure 6, which shows an example of a simple network and a multitiered network with a top, middle, and bottom tier.

TIERING TERMINOLOGY

Flow-through Entity: An entity for which income is allocated by the business to its owners, with taxes on that income paid only by the owners. Taxes generally are not paid by the flow-through entities themselves. Flow-through entities include partnerships, S corporations, trusts, and estates.

Ultimate Owner: A final recipient of flow-through income allocations. Ultimate owners include nonflow-through businesses (e.g., tax-exempt entities and C corporations) and individuals.

Simple Network: A network that includes a flow-through entity that does not receive allocations from another flow-through entity or allocate income to another flow-through entity. It allocates income to ultimate owners.

Multitiered Network: A network that includes at least one flow-through entity that allocates income to another flow-through entity.

Enterprise: A network of flow-through entities and their owners whose economic activity is under the control (defined as 50 percent or more direct or indirect ownership) of a single taxpayer or married couple.

Top-tier Entity: A flow-through entity that allocates income to another flow-through entity (and possibly also to ultimate owners) but does not receive allocations from another flow-through entity.

Middle-tier Entity: A flow-through entity that both receives allocations from another flow-through entity and allocates income to another flow-through entity (and possibly also to ultimate owners).

Bottom-tier Entity: A flow-through entity that receives allocations from another flow-through entity, but does not allocate income to another flow-through entity. It allocates income to ultimate owners.

Source: GAO analysis of IRS documents.

S Corporations Have Shallow Tiering Depths, while Some Partnerships Have Greater Depths

In tax year 2011, only about 1 percent of S corporations had 2 or more tiers below them (see table 3). More partnerships, on the other hand, had greater tiering depths. About 23 percent of partnerships had 2 or more tiers below them, and some partnerships had 11 or more tiers below them. [46] See figure 6 above for examples of how tiers below flow-through entities are counted.

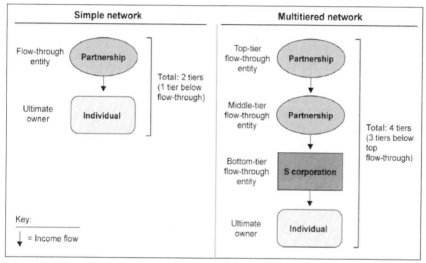

Source: GAO analysis of IRS information.

Figure 6. A Simple Network and a Multitiered Network.

Most Ultimate Owners Are Individuals

Most ultimate owners of partnerships and S corporations are individuals. This ownership structure is the most simple. Structures with ultimate owners that are businesses are more complex because the businesses, in turn, are controlled by other entities.

For example, C corporations are controlled by their boards and shareholders.

Most partnerships and S corporations were owned exclusively by individuals in tax year 2011. S corporations' ownership was simplest, with 97 percent of all S corporations owned exclusively by individuals. Partnerships showed greater complexity, with 77 percent of all partnerships owned exclusively by individuals and 22 percent owned by mixed types of owners. [47] The types of owners for partnerships and S corporations in tax year 2011 are shown in table 4.

Table 3. Number of Tiers below Partnerships and S Corporations, Tax Year 2011

Tiers below entity	Partnerships	S corporations
	Approximate number of entities	
1 (ultimate owners only)	2,604,000	4,201,000
2-10	778,000	35,000
11+	Less than 1,000	Less than 1%
Total	**3,382,000**	**4,237,000**
	Percentage of entities	
1 (ultimate owners only)	77%	99%
2-10	23%	1%
11+	Less than 1%	Less than 1%
Total	**100%**	**100%**

Source: GAO analysis of IRS data.

Notes: Because the K-1 database does not have complete K-1 data, the extent of tiering presented in this figure represents a minimum amount, and counts are approximate.

Columns may not sum to totals due to rounding.

This table measures only the number of tiers below a given entity, not the number of tiers that might be above it, because the focus of this table is each partnership's and S corporation's investment structure. This means that the table does not show whether the partnership or S corporation is itself part of the investment structure of another flow-through entity, and therefore does not necessarily show whether it is part of multitiered network.

Most Partnerships and S Corporations Have 1 to 2 Ultimate Owners, but Many Have 11 or More

Another factor in the complexity of a flow-through entity is the number of ultimate owners (see the text box above for a definition of ultimate owners). As shown in figure 7, most S corporations are closely held, i.e., owned by a small number of ultimate owners. In tax year 2011, 62 percent had only one ultimate owner, and an additional 28 percent had only two ultimate owners. Partnerships tend to have more ultimate owners. In tax year 2011, 51 percent had 2 ultimate owners, 38 percent had 3 to 10 ultimate owners, and 9 percent had 11 or more ultimate owners.

Table 4. Types of Ultimate Owners of Partnerships and S Corporations, Tax Year 2011

Type of owner	Partnerships	S corporations
	Approximate number	
Only individuals who filed tax returns	2,597,000	4,118,000
Only businesses that filed tax returns	23,000	10,000
Only individuals, businesses, and other entities that did not file tax returns[a]	24,000	28,000
Mix of the above categories	738,000	80,000
Total	**3,382,000**	**4,237,000**
	Percent	
Only individuals who filed tax returns	77%	97%
Only businesses that filed tax returns	1%	0%
Only individuals, businesses, and other entities that did not file tax returns[a]	1%	1%
Mix of the above categories	22%	2%
Total	**100%**	**100%**

Source: GAO analysis of IRS data.

Notes: Because the K-1 database does not have complete K-1 data, entity counts are approximate.

Columns may not sum to totals due to rounding.

[a] Entities not filing tax returns include legitimate nonfilers such as business subsidiaries and individuals not required to file. They may also include nonfilers who should be filing and parties with invalid taxpayer identification numbers.

Most Enterprises Are Simple, but Some Are Multitiered with Many Component Entities

Most enterprises (see text box above for definition) are simple and have few component entities, but some are multitiered and have large numbers of component entities (see figure 8). Enterprises are of particular interest to IRS because controlling owners have the ability to influence activity throughout the network. In tax year 2011, about 62 percent of enterprises had two tiers—i.e., they were simple networks—and were composed of about four entities on average (counting both flow-through entities and ultimate owners).[48] About 35 percent of enterprises had three tiers and were composed of about five entities on average. In comparison, the seven enterprises that were nine or more tiers deep were composed of about 735 entities on average.

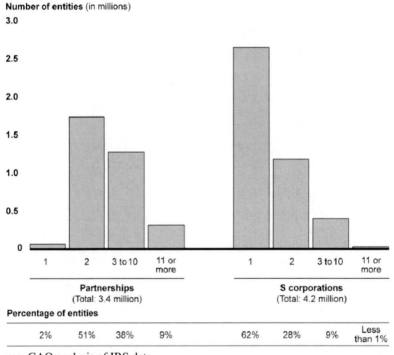

Source: GAO analysis of IRS data.

Notes:

Because the K-1 database does not have complete K-1 data, the extent of tiering presented in this figure represents a minimum amount, and entity counts are approximate.

Percentages for S corporations do not sum to 100 percent due to rounding.

Figure 7. Number of Ultimate Owners for Partnerships and S Corporations, Tax Year 2011.

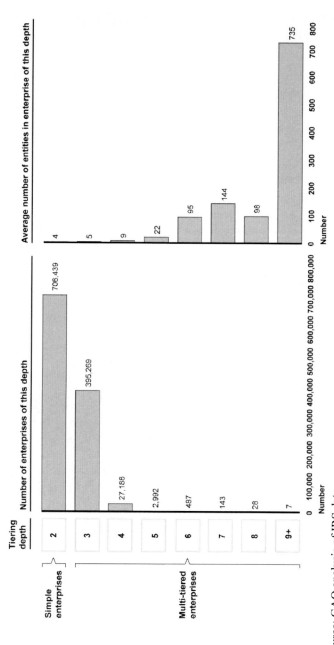

Source: GAO analysis of IRS data.

Notes: Because the K-1 database does not have complete K-1 data, the extent of tiering presented in this figure represents a minimum amount, and entity counts are approximate.

Averages for numbers of entities include both flow-through entities and ultimate owners.

Figure 8. Number of Enterprises and Average Number of Entities per Enterprise, by Tiering Depth, Tax Year 2011.

APPENDIX III. ADDITIONAL INFORMATION
ABOUT MISREPORTING

Methodology for Estimating Individuals' Total Misreporting of Income from Partnerships and S Corporations

The Internal Revenue Service (IRS) estimated that individual taxpayers misreported, in net terms, 15 percent of the total income from partnerships and S corporations that they should have reported on their tax returns.[49] This percentage is known as the net misreporting percentage (see figure 9).

We calculated the total income that should have been reported—$606 billion—from the IRS's National Research Program (NRP) data on individual taxpayer compliance as the sum of the absolute values of the income amounts that individual taxpayers should have reported. Absolute values are used in calculating the amount of income that should have been reported to prevent negative income amounts from canceling out positive income amounts. Based on these figures, we estimated that in tax years 2006 through 2009, individual taxpayers reported about $91 billion less per year in net income from partnerships and S corporations than they actually were allocated. To arrive at the $91 billion estimate, we adjusted upward based on IRS's 15 percent misreporting percentage estimate from a raw estimate of $27 billion.[50]

There is some uncertainty with both IRS's estimated net misreporting percentage and the amount of total income from partnerships and S corporations individual taxpayers should have reported. IRS arrived at an estimate of 15 percent for the net misreporting percentage by adjusting upward the net misreporting percentage based on raw data from its NRP. In NRP, IRS selects a random sample of individual tax returns each year to examine and strives to verify information taxpayers reported or should have reported. The net misreporting percentage based directly on NRP data was 4.5 percent for income allocated to individuals by partnerships and S corporations. According to IRS officials, this was probably an understatement because it did not include misreporting undetected by IRS examiners or possible misreporting at the flow-through entity level carried through to individual taxpayers. Based on an IRS study of S corporation (but not partnership) returns from 2003 and 2004, IRS officials said that the net misreporting percentage for income from both partnerships and S corporations for tax years 2006 through 2009 was probably around 15 percent. IRS used only the S corporation study to arrive at the 15 percent because it has not conducted a similar study of partnerships in recent years. We cannot know whether the estimate might have been higher or lower if partnerships were taken into account. Each of the factors mentioned here—undetected individual misreporting, entity-level misreporting, the age of the data in the S corporation study, and the lack of information on partnerships—creates some uncertainty about the 15 percent estimate.

Because of the uncertainty related to IRS's net misreporting percentage, there is also uncertainty about our estimate for net misreported amount. Additionally, the confidence interval around the raw NRP estimate translates to a larger confidence interval for the adjusted estimate. Likewise, in calculating net misreported income, we considered only partnership and S corporation income that was separately reported on Form 1040's Schedule E, *Supplemental Income and Loss*. Some income from partnerships and S corporations may also be included within, and reported under, other line items on Form 1040, such as capital gains.

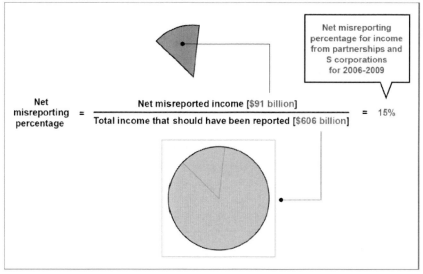

Note:

    The numerator is the sum of all amounts underreported minus the sum of all amounts overreported on an item, such as income allocated from partnerships and S corporations. The denominator is the sum of the absolute values of the amounts that should have been reported on that item. Absolute values are used for the denominator to prevent negative income amounts from canceling out positive income amounts.

Figure 9. What Net Misreporting Percentage Means.

IRS has not issued its own estimate of misreporting of partnership and S corporation income for 2006 or later. Our estimate of lost tax revenue cannot be used to compute a tax gap estimate (defined by IRS as the amount of tax liability faced by taxpayers that is not paid on time), as IRS may perform additional adjustments for its tax gap estimates.

To calculate the amount of taxes that corresponded to our misreporting estimate, we used NRP data to calculate the income and misreporting that related to individuals with different effective tax rates (defined as total tax divided by adjusted gross income). From 2006 to 2009, taxpayers with effective tax rates of less than 15 percent had an aggregate annual net loss on income from partnerships and S corporations, while taxpayers with effective tax rates of 15 percent or higher had aggregate net income. The highest tax bracket was 35 percent. Looking at taxpayers with effective tax rates between 15 and 35 percent, and using the minimum and maximum tax rates within each effective tax rate grouping and point estimates for misreporting, we calculated lower and upper bounds for the amount of tax that would have been owed on their misreported income from partnerships and S corporations. With this, we arrived at an estimate of $5 billion to $6 billion. Adjusting our point estimate for taxes based on the same methodology discussed above for our misreporting estimate, we arrived at an estimated $19 billion in taxes owed on the misreported income.

Comparison of Individual Misreporting of Income from S Corporations and Partnerships with Misreporting of Other Income Types

There are several ways to compare the extent and nature of misreporting of partnership and S corporation income with individuals' misreporting of other types of income, which are shown in table 5.[51] To compare net misreporting of income from partnerships and S corporations with other types of income, we needed to use unadjusted data, because IRS had not issued adjusted results for 2006 or later at the level of detail needed for the table. For example, the unadjusted net misreporting amount for partnership and S corporation income shown in the table is $27 billion, as opposed to the adjusted amount of $91 billion.

Table 5. Individual Taxpayers' Misreporting of Income, Annual Average for Tax Years 2006-2009

Income type	Total reported net income (billions of dollars)[a]	Net misreporting (billions of dollars)[a]	Net misreporting adjusted for undetected misreporting (billions of dollars)[a]	Percent of taxpayers misreporting this income type[a]	Amount of information reporting required (per IRS)[c]
BUSINESS INCOME					
Partnership and S corporation income	$395 (+/-14%)	$27[b] (+/-21%)	$91[b]	23%	Some
Sole proprietor income	256	152	Not estimated	74	Little or none
Rental real estate and royalties	Omitted	27 (+/-12%)	Not estimated	62	Little or none
Estate and trust income	17 (+/-29%)	Omitted	Not estimated	8	Some
Farm income	-13 (+/-26%)	10 (+/-14%)	Not estimated	77	Little or none
NON BUSINESS INCOME (largest categories based on total income)					
Wages	5,545	11 (+/-29%)	Not estimated	6	Substantial
Capital gains	493 (+/-25%)	28 (+/-29%)	Not estimated	25	Some
Pensions	460	Omitted	Not estimated	10	Substantial
Interest		189	3 (+/-29%)	Not estimated	22 Substantial
Dividends		176	Omitted	Not estimated	21 Substantial
Taxable Social Security		158	6 (+/-18%)	Not estimated	27 Substantial

Source: GAO analysis of IRS data.

Notes:

[a] Results for dollar estimates with relative margins of error greater than plus or minus 30 percent are omitted, and relative margins of error greater than plus or minus 10 percent are listed in parentheses. All other dollar estimates are within plus or minus 10 percent of the reported values. All percentage estimates have relative margins of error within plus or minus 10 percentage points of the reported values. Due to non-sampling error related to the uncertainty about undetected misreporting, actual amounts of net misreporting may be outside of those margins. The unadjusted net misreporting numbers in this table represent a minimum, according to IRS. See the discussion above the table for further discussion.

[b] According to IRS officials, the net misreporting percentage we calculated based on National Research Program data (4.5 percent) is probably an understatement. Based on the results of its 2003–4 study of S corporations, IRS officials estimated that the true net misreporting percentage for 2006 was closer to 15 percent, and, using this percentage, we calculated the 2006-9 net misreporting amount to be about $91 billion. While IRS officials have not issued similar estimates, they said that the same reasoning they used for 2006, discussed above in this report, would also apply for 2007 through 2009.

[c] This column refers to information provided by third parties to IRS. The amount can be substantial in the case of W-2s for wages paid to individuals, some as for K-1s, and little or none for business income earned by sole proprietors.

In general, frequency of misreporting of income from partnerships and S corporations was lower than for income from sole proprietorships, and higher than for misreporting of income from nonbusiness sources. There is a general pattern in misreporting of income. The more third-party information reporting there is for a type of income (such as W-2s for wages), the less misreporting there is for that type of income (see table 5). According to IRS, information reporting increases voluntary tax compliance because taxpayers know that IRS is aware of their income. For example, employer information on wages and earnings is sent both to employees and to IRS, and for tax years 2006 through 2009, the net misreporting percentage for wages was less than 1 percent.

Partnerships and S corporations send partners, shareholders, and IRS Schedules K-1 that state the amount of income distributed to each partner or shareholder. In comparison, most other types of business income earned by individuals are covered by little to no information reporting. However, according to IRS officials, many partnerships and S corporations issuing K-1s are closely held, i.e., controlled by the individual taxpayers receiving the K-1s. In these cases, the information on the K-1 does not truly come from an unrelated third party.

APPENDIX IV. ADDITIONAL INFORMATION ABOUT K-1 MATCHING

K-1 Matching Is Complicated for Several Reasons

Schedule K-1 reporting is complex for several reasons:

- Some taxpayers with K-1 income have K-1s from multiple partnerships and S corporations, which adds complexity. For example, a taxpayer may net the income/loss amounts from different K-1s, so that the netted amount reported on the 1040 will not match the individual K-1s, but correct information may turn out to be contained within the netted numbers, according to IRS officials.
- One tax return preparer we interviewed noted that when tiered networks are involved (e.g., partnerships that have other partnerships as partners), each tier must wait for the tier above it to send its K-1s in order to have accurate information, yet they all have the same filing deadline. If the top-tier entity sends its K-1s close to the deadline, the

lower tiers must estimate the amounts to put on their own K-1s in order to file on time. This can lead to inaccuracies and mismatches.

- When taxpayers respond to notices about mismatches, IRS guidance directs AUR reviewers to consider the reasonableness of taxpayers' responses, but reviewers generally do not examine the accuracy of the information in the responses because they do not have examination authority.

- K-1 matching is only designed to detect noncompliance at the taxpayer level, not at the entity level. According to an IRS official, because many partnerships and S corporations issuing K-1s are controlled by the individual taxpayers receiving the K-1s, the information on K-1s may match what is on the Forms 1040 but still understate taxes owed.

Because of issues like these, K-1 matching is only part of IRS's efforts to ensure compliance with tax rules about income from partnerships and S corporations. Examinations, discussed previously, also play a role.

Individual Tax Returns with Partnership and S Corporation K-1 Mismatches Had Higher Screen-out and No-Change Rates Than All Returns in IRS's Matching Program

The screen-out rate (percent of returns reviewed without taxpayer contact) and the no-change rate (percent of taxpayers contacted that did not result in an assessment) for K-1 matching for tax year 2009, the latest year for which complete data were available, were higher than for the Automated Underreporter (AUR) program overall (AUR matches 1040s with many information documents, including K-1s). As shown in figure 10, about 61 percent of the returns with partnership and S corporation K-1 mismatches in IRS's AUR workload were screened out.[52] That is, the AUR examiner determined that despite the mismatch, the taxpayer was in compliance with tax law or within a small tolerance threshold (i.e., income or expenses were misreported by an amount below what IRS considers productive to address), and the AUR examiner did not contact the taxpayer. In contrast, about 18 percent of all returns in the total AUR workload were screened out. Of the partnership and S corporation mismatch cases where IRS contacted a taxpayer, the no-change rate was about 58 percent. In contrast, the no-change rate for all of AUR was about 19 percent.

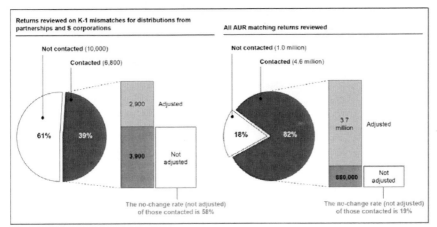

Source: GAO analysis of IRS data.

Notes:

> Schedules K-1 are information returns that partnerships and S corporations are required to send to each of their partners and shareholders, respectively, reporting how much income or loss they allocated to that partner or shareholder in the past year. They also send a copy to IRS.

Numbers may not match up precisely due to rounding.

Figure 10. Case Processing Results for Partnership and S Corporation Mismatches Involving Schedules K-1 and All AUR Mismatches, Tax Year 2009 (Percentages and Numbers of Returns).

End Notes

[1] An S corporation is a corporation meeting certain requirements that elects to be taxed under subchapter S of the Internal Revenue Code.

[2] The year 2008 is the most recent for which IRS compiled complete data comparing gross receipts for all business types.

[3] Estates and trusts are also flow-through entities. However, in tax year 2011, the most recent year for which complete data are available, partnerships and S corporations accounted for about 96 percent of net flow-through income (positive income minus losses) reported by individuals.

[4] Individuals, corporations, trusts, estates, tax-exempt entities, and other partnerships may all be partners in a partnership. Individuals, certain trusts, estates, and certain tax-exempt entities may be shareholders in an S corporation. See 26 U.S.C. § 1361(b)(1)(B).

[5] The returns that partnerships and S corporations file with IRS are the Form 1065, *U.S. Return of Partnership Income*, and the Form 1120S, *U.S. Income Tax Return for an S Corporation*, respectively.

[6] GAO, *Using Data from the Internal Revenue Service's National Research Program to Identify Potential Opportunities to Reduce the Tax Gap*, GAO-07-423R (Washington, D.C.: Mar. 15, 2007).

[7] For more information about tax evasion by networks, see GAO, *Tax Gap: IRS Can Improve Efforts to Address Tax Evasion by Networks of Businesses and Related Entities,* GAO-10-968 (Washington, D.C.: Sept. 24, 2010).

[8] Partnerships and S corporations use Schedule K-1 to report to partners, shareholders, and IRS a partner's or shareholder's share of income, losses, credits, and deductions.

[9] GAO, *Tax Administration: IRS' Partnership Compliance Activities Could Be Improved,* GAO/GGD-95-151 (Washington, D.C.: June 16, 1995); TIGTA, *Despite Some Favorable Partnership Audit Trends, the Number of No-Change Audits Is a Concern,* 2012-30-60 (Washington, D.C.: June 20, 2012); *The Recommended Adjustments from S Corporation Audits Are Substantial, but the Number of No-Change Audits Is a Concern,* 2012-30-62 (Washington, D.C.: June 21, 2012).

[10] See 26 U.S.C. § 1361(b)(1)(B).

[11] Gross business receipts do not include portfolio income or income from other flow-through entities.

[12] 26 U.S.C. §§ 6031, 6037; 26 C.F.R. §§ 1.6031(a)-1, 1.6037-1.

[13] In general, income types that are subject to higher levels of information reporting show higher levels of taxpayer compliance.

[14] Business entities are also allocated income by partnerships and S corporations. We have focused this analysis on individuals.

[15] IRS did not publish the results of this study. Selected results from the study were presented at the 2009 IRS Research Conference, held on July 8, 2009.

[16] IRS generally adjusts its research examination estimates on individual noncompliance to account for examiners not having all of the necessary information with respect to circumstances surrounding taxpayers' true reporting obligations, and examiners' differing abilities to detect noncompliance. It does so by quantifying the extent to which examination results depend on who conducted the examination, essentially constructing a statistical profile of the theoretical best examiner possible. IRS officials told us that constructing such a model for the S corporation study was not possible because the study did not collect unique identifiers specifying which examiner worked on each return.

[17] Relative margins of error for all estimates are less than plus or minus 10 percent unless otherwise noted. However, due to non-sampling error related to the uncertainty about undetected misreporting, actual amounts may be outside of those margins. Approximately 25 percent of the returns used for the S corporation study were from tax year 2003 and 75 percent from tax year 2004. All numbers we report based on the study use a corresponding weighted average of results from the two years.

[18] Throughout this report, we use the term double counted to refer to items that are counted two or more times (not necessarily exactly two times).

[19] A total of $1,468 billion was reported by partnerships with positive values for total income (losses) after subtracting deductions. A total of negative $507 billion was reported by partnerships with negative values for total income (losses) after subtracting deductions.

[20] See appendix I for discussion of the data source and data limitations of our estimates about multitiered networks.

[21] GAO, *Tax Gap: IRS Could Significantly Increase Revenues by Better Targeting Enforcement Resources,* GAO-13-151 (Washington, D.C.: Dec. 5, 2012).

[22] The relative margin of error for this estimate is under plus or minus 10 percent. However, due to non-sampling error related to the uncertainty about undetected misreporting, the actual amount may be outside of those margins.

[23] Ordinary business income is the income a business earns from its own trade or business activities.

[24] For example, interest passed through from partnerships and S corporations and interest from nonflow-through sources are both reported on line 8a of Form 1040.

[25] We estimated that individual taxpayers with positive values for income (losses) from partnerships and S corporations had an annual average total of $517 billion of such income

(with a relative margin of error of plus or minus 10.1 percent), and that individual taxpayers with negative values for income (losses) from partnerships and S corporations had an annual average total of negative $94 billion of such income (with a relative margin of error of 20.2 percent). The net of $423 billion has a relative margin of error of 13.3 percent.

[26] An unknown amount of the income misreported by individuals resulted from individuals reporting a different amount of income to IRS than they actually were allocated by partnerships and S corporations, while the partnerships and S corporations reported the correct amount to IRS. Another unknown amount resulted from the partnerships and S corporations reporting their own income incorrectly to IRS, which (as mentioned already) should be reflected in misreporting by the ultimate taxpayers.

[27] We focused on revenue agent examinations of partnerships and S corporations because tax compliance officers conduct very few examinations of these entities. In general, revenue agents conduct examinations of more complex tax returns including partnerships and corporations, while tax compliance officers primarily conduct examinations of individual taxpayers.

[28] Fiscal years 2011 and 2012 were the two most recent years of data available at the time we did our analysis.

[29] From 2006 to 2009, taxpayers with effective tax rates of less than 15 percent had an aggregate annual net loss on income from partnerships and S corporations, while taxpayers with effective tax rates of 15 percent or higher had aggregate net income.

[30] Adjustments in AUR cannot be pinpointed precisely for any of the income or expense categories tracked. An evaluation of whether it would be worthwhile for IRS to keep these data a different way is outside the scope of this work, as it would require an analysis of the AUR program as a whole.

[31] GAO, *Tax Administration: IRS Could Improve Examinations by Adopting Certain Research Program Practices*, GAO-13-480 (Washington, D.C.: May 24, 2013).

[32] An IRS official noted that some partnership and S corporation returns may be marked as not changed although the examination resulted in changes at the partner or shareholder level.

[33] Filters are flags that detect certain characteristics.

[34] GAO, *E-filing Tax Returns: Penalty Authority and Digitizing More Paper Return Data Could Increase Benefits*, GAO-12-33 (Washington, D.C.: Oct. 5, 2011).

[35] 26 U.S.C. § 6011(e)(2) and 26 C.F.R. § 301.6011-5. In addition, current law generally prohibits requiring e-filing by individuals, estates, and trusts, unless the return is prepared and filed by a tax return preparer who reasonably expects to prepare more than 10 individual tax returns during the calendar year. 26 U.S.C. § 6011(e)(1) and (e)(3).

[36] 26 U.S.C. § 6011(e)(2)(B). When requiring e-filing, the ability of taxpayers to comply at reasonable cost must be considered, among other relevant factors.

[37] For instance, IRS projected that 80 percent of partnerships would e-file in fiscal year 2015 and 86 percent in fiscal year 2020. According to IRS officials, the projections were based on processing activity. Processing activity refers to everything related to a particular return that goes through IRS in a given processing year. For instance, if two, three, or four iterations of a tax return go through IRS, the return is counted two, three, or four times. Actual e-filing percentages mentioned here count each return only once.

[38] As an example of the difference that a mandate on the basis of a balance sheet could make, requiring e-filing by partnerships required to file a balance sheet—generally those with $500,000 or more in assets and $250,000 or more in receipts—would have covered about 75 percent of partnerships in tax year 2011. The 64 percent of partnerships that actually e-filed in tax year 2011 presumably included some partnerships with lower levels of assets or receipts.

[39] The DIF model is a mathematical technique used to score income tax returns for examination potential.

[40] GAO/GGD-95-151.

[41] TIGTA, 2012-30-60, 2012-30-62.

[42] GAO/GGD-95-151; TIGTA, 2012-30-60; 2012-30-062.

[43] From 2006 to 2009, taxpayers with effective tax rates of less than 15 percent had an aggregate annual net loss on income from partnerships and S corporations, while taxpayers with effective tax rates of 15 percent or higher had aggregate net income; the highest tax bracket was 35 percent.

[44] GAO, *Tax Administration: IRS' Partnership Compliance Activities Could Be Improved,* GAO/GGD-95-151 (Washington, D.C.: June 16, 1995); TIGTA, *Despite Some Favorable Partnership Audit Trends, the Number of No-Change Audits Is a Concern,* 2012-30-060 (Washington, D.C.: June 20, 2012); *The Recommended Adjustments From S Corporation Audits Are Substantial, but the Number of No-Change Audits Is a Concern,* 2012-30-062 (Washington, D.C.: June 21, 2012).

[45] GAO, *Tax Gap: IRS Can Improve Efforts to Address Tax Evasion by Networks of Businesses and Related Entities,* GAO-10-968 (Washington, D.C.: Sept. 24, 2010).

[46] This discussion centers on the number of tiers below a given entity, not the number of tiers that might be above it, because the focus is each partnership's and S corporation's investment structure. This means that these numbers do not indicate whether a partnership or S corporation is itself part of the investment structure of another flow-through entity, and therefore do not necessarily indicate whether it is part of a multitiered network. Because of this, these numbers do not match the numbers shown previously in figure 4.

[47] About 1 percent of both partnerships and S corporations had ultimate owners that did not file tax returns in tax year 2011. These may have been individuals or businesses, and they may have been excused from filing or may not have filed when they should have filed.

[48] As illustrated above in figure 6, networks with only two tiers do not have any flow-through entities passing income to other flow-through entities, so they are not considered multitiered networks.

[49] Relative margins of error for all estimates are less than plus or minus 10 percent unless otherwise noted. However, due to non-sampling error related to the uncertainty about undetected misreporting, actual amounts may be outside of those margins.

[50] The raw net misreported income amount based on NRP data was $27 billion, with a relative margin of error of plus or minus 21.0 percent. However, due to non-sampling error related to the uncertainty about undetected misreporting, the actual amount may be outside of those margins.

[51] We included the business income category types that are listed on the front of Form 1040, and the business income subcategories listed on Schedule E of Form 1040, with absolute values for total reported income greater than $10 billion. We also calculated total reported income for all nonbusiness income categories on the front of Form 1040 and included the six categories with absolute values of reported incomes of more than $150 billion each in our comparisons.

[52] Because of resource issues, IRS selects only a portion of K-1 mismatches for inclusion in the workload.

In: Partnerships and S Corporations
Editor: Keith Preston

ISBN: 978-1-63463-124-2
© 2014 Nova Science Publishers, Inc.

Chapter 2

WHO EARNS PASS-THROUGH BUSINESS INCOME? AN ANALYSIS OF INDIVIDUAL TAX RETURN DATA[*]

Mark P. Keightley

SUMMARY

Pass-through businesses — sole proprietorships, partnerships, and S corporations — generate more than half of all business income in the United States. Pass-through income is, in general, taxed only once at the individual income tax rates when it is distributed to its owners. In contrast, the income of C corporations is taxed twice; once at the corporate level according to corporate tax rates, and then a second time at the individual tax rates when shareholders receive dividend payments or realize capital gains. This leads to the so-called ""double taxation"" of corporate profits.

This report analyzes individual tax return data to determine who earns pass-through business income and bears the burden of taxes on that income. The analysis finds that over 82% of net pass-through income is earned by taxpayers with an adjusted gross income (AGI) over $100,000, although these taxpayers account for just 23% of returns filed. A significant fraction of pass-through income is concentrated among upper-

---

[*] This is an edited, reformatted and augmented version of a Congressional Research Service publication, CRS Report for Congress R42359, from www.crs.gov, prepared for Members and Committees of Congress, dated February 16, 2012.

income earners. Taxpayers with AGI over $250,000, for example, receive 62% of pass-through income, but account for just over 6% of returns with pass-through income. A closer look at S corporations and partnerships shows passive income accounts for 10% and 25%, respectively, of their total income. This analysis, when combined with research on the corporate tax burden, suggests that higher-income taxpayers will generally bear most of the burden from increased pass-through taxes.

A number of proposed and scheduled tax changes would result in pass-throughs paying higher taxes. Several lawmakers and the Obama Administration, for example, have expressed interest in taxing large pass-throughs as corporations, which would subject some pass-throughs to an additional layer of taxation. Pass-through taxation could also increase if a tax reform that includes lower corporate tax rates that are paid for by the elimination or reduction of certain business tax benefits is enacted. Additionally, the scheduled expiration of the 2001/2003 tax cuts at the end of this year could increase taxes on pass-throughs by increasing individual tax rates. Lastly, a new 3.8% tax on passive income that was enacted as part of the Health Care and Education Reconciliation Act of 2010 (HCERA, P.L. 111-152) is set to take effect in 2013. The tax may apply to some pass-throughs.

While the analysis of these proposed and scheduled changes suggests that higher-income taxpayers will generally bear most of the burden from increased pass-through taxes, there are circumstances that could raise congressional concern. For example, an across-the-board expiration of the 2001/2003 individual tax rates will increase taxes for all pass-through owners. One option for preventing the tax burden from increasing for lower and middle class business owners is to allow the reduced rates to expire only for higher-income earners.

Concern has also risen over the new 3.8% tax on passive income and its effect on pass-throughs. The distributional analysis in this report shows, however, most S corporation and partnership income is the active type, and active business income is exempt from the 3.8% tax. The share of income that is passive, and potentially subject to the new tax, overwhelmingly accrues to higher-income taxpayers — 77% of passive partnership income and 93% of passive S corporation income went to taxpayers with AGI over $250,000. Sole proprietors could generally be expected to be exempt from the tax since most of their income is likely active.

INTRODUCTION

More than half of business income is generated by sole proprietorships, partnerships, and S corporations.[1] This fact is important because the income of these businesses is, in general, taxed only once at the individual income tax rates when it is distributed to its owners. This has led sole proprietorships, partnerships, and S corporations to be referred to as ""pass-throughs"" since their income ""passes through"" the business to its owners.[2] In contrast, the income of C corporations is taxed twice; once at the corporate level according to corporate tax rates, and then a second time at the individual tax rates when shareholders receive dividend payments or realize capital gains. This leads to the so-called ""double taxation"" of corporate profits.[3]

A number of proposed and scheduled tax changes could result in pass-throughs paying higher taxes. Several lawmakers and the Obama Administration, for example, have expressed interest in taxing large pass-throughs as corporations, which would subject some of these entities to an additional layer of taxation. Pass-through taxation could also increase if one of the proposed tax reform plans that call for lower corporate tax rates paid for by the elimination or reduction of certain business tax benefits is enacted. Additionally, the scheduled expiration of the 2001/2003 tax cuts at the end of this year could increase taxes on pass-throughs. Lastly, a new 3.8% "unearned income Medicare contribution" tax that is set to take effect in 2013 may apply to some pass-throughs.

This report uses a nationally representative sample of tax returns to analyze who earns pass-through income.[4] The analysis finds that upper-income earners account for the majority of pass-through income earned, although lower- and middle-income taxpayers account for the majority of pass-through returns filed. The analysis then determines who would bear the burden of increased taxes on pass-throughs. Theoretically, it is possible that higher-income pass-through owners could shift the burden of increased taxes to lower- and middle-income employees by reducing wages or employment. The analysis on who earns pass-through income, when combined with research on the corporate tax burden, however, suggests that most of the tax burden would fall on higher-income taxpayers. A more detailed discussion of the proposed and scheduled tax changes is presented before moving on to the analysis.

PROPOSED AND SCHEDULED TAX CHANGES

A number of recent proposals could increase taxes for pass-throughs. In early 2011, Senate Finance Committee Chairman Max Baucus suggested, for example, that pass-throughs earning above a certain income might have to be taxed as corporations.[5] That same year, while testifying before the Senate Finance Committee, Treasury Secretary Tim Geithner said "Congress has to revisit this basic question about whether it makes sense for us as a country to allow certain businesses to choose whether they're treated as corporations for tax purposes or not.""[6] The Treasury Secretary's comments seemed to indicate his concern about large pass-throughs that were paying lower taxes by intentionally choosing not to be taxed as a corporation. The Secretary''s comments also appear to resonate with reports that the Administration is developing a proposal to tax large pass-throughs as corporations, as well as consistent with a broad proposal made by the President''s Economic Recovery Advisory Board to tax pass-throughs with corporate characteristics as corporations.[7]

Recent proposals by lawmakers and the Administration to reform the corporate tax code have called for lower corporate tax rates paid for by the elimination or reduction of certain corporate tax benefits, which could affect pass-throughs.[8] Pass-throughs would generally not benefit from a reduction in corporate tax rates, since their income is not subject to the corporate tax. Additionally, depending on how corporate tax benefits are scaled back to offset a rate reduction, pass-throughs could see their tax burden increase. The reason is that not all ""corporate"" tax benefits are exclusively available to corporations. Often they are available to business more generally.[9]

Scheduled tax changes that could potentially affect pass-throughs include the expiration of the 2001/2003 tax cuts, later extended in 2010, that is set to occur at the end of 2012. Specifically, barring congressional action, the current individual tax rate structure of 10%, 15% 25%, 28%, 33%, and 35% will revert to 15%, 28%, 31%, 36%, and 39.6%. Since ordinary pass-through income is taxed according to individual rates, some owners of pass-through businesses would likely experience an increase in taxes owed.[10] A number of pass-through business owners who realize capital gains, including hedge fund managers who realize carried interest income, could also see taxes increase if the reduced rates for long-term capital gains are also allowed to expire.[11]

The other scheduled tax change that may affect pass-throughs is a new 3.8% "unearned income Medicare contribution"" tax set to take effect in 2013.[12] Specifically, the Health Care and Education Reconciliation Act of

2010 (HCERA, P.L. 111-152) included a 3.8% tax on the passive income of those with incomes over $250,000 (couples) and $200,000 (singles). The tax is limited to the excess of income over these amounts or total passive income, whichever is smaller. Active business income is excluded from the tax. There is concern in the business community that this tax may negatively affect pass-through business owners who earn passive business income.[13]

WHO EARNS PASS-THROUGH BUSINESS INCOME?

Approximately 27 million (or one in five) taxpayers reported pass-through business income (or loss) totaling more than $704 billion in 2006. Among those earning pass-through income, the average amount reported was $26,011. These figures exclude capital gains income from passthroughs and farming income. This section analyzes the distribution of pass-through income by a measure of taxpayer income that is used for tax purposes — adjusted gross income (AGI). When useful and possible, the analysis also distinguishes between sole proprietorship, partnership, and S corporation income, as well as active and passive income.

Figure 1 shows the distribution of pass-through income by AGI class. A more detailed distribution, along with the distribution of tax returns reporting pass-through income, may be found in *Table A-1* of the *Appendix*. Taxpayers with income of $100,000 or greater earned 82% of pass-through income, while accounting for roughly 23% of returns reporting pass-through income. Conversely, taxpayers with AGI less than $100,000 earned about 18% of pass-through income, but accounted for 77% of returns with pass-through income. A significant proportion of pass-through income was concentrated among upper-income earners. Taxpayers with AGI over $250,000, for example, received 62% of pass-through income, but accounted for just over 6% of returns reporting such income. Millionaires earned about 35% of pass-through income, while filing roughly 1% of all returns with pass-through income.

Table 1 displays the distribution of pass-through income by business type. The distribution shows that sole proprietorship income was more evenly distributed across income groups than partnership and S corporation income. Partnership net income was more concentrated among upper income individuals with nearly all of it accruing to taxpayers with AGI in excess of $100,000, including nearly 44% accruing to those with AGI over $1 million. S corporation income was also concentrated at the upper-end of the distribution, although more so than partnership income. For example, while nearly all of S corporation income accrued to taxpayers with income over $100,000, a greater share went to those with AGI over $1 million than with partnership income — about 58%.

Table 1 also shows a concentration of net losses for partnerships and S corporations at the lower end of the income distribution. Pass-through income and losses are one component of AGI. Thus, if a taxpayer relies primarily on a partnership or S corporation for income, and the business realizes losses, the taxpayer's AGI will likely be negative.

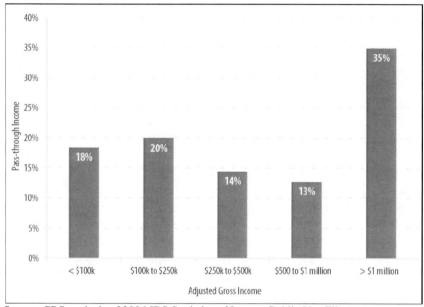

Source: CRS analysis of 2006 IRS Statistics of Income Public Use Files.

Figure 1. Distribution of Net Pass-Through Income by AGI, 2006.

There are several scenarios which could explain the losses. A portion of these losses may be due to start-up business that are experiencing losses. It is also possible that a portion of these losses are due to failing businesses, both new and old. Lastly, some of the losses may be attributable to temporary business disruptions experienced at particular firms. Without more detailed data on the businesses associated with these losses, however, its difficult to know for certain. The individual data do show that for most taxpayers at this end of the distribution, partnership and S corporation losses were larger than non pass-through income, indicating that these taxpayers were relying primarily on pass-through income. Partnership and S corporation income can be separated into active and passive income. The distinction between the two can be important because passive activity losses rules generally prevent passive losses from offsetting active income. Active income is income resulting from active participation in a business, whereas passive income is income from a business that the taxpayer did not materially participate in. A business partner involved in the day to day management and operations of the business, for example, would earn active income, while a silent partner who has no involvement in the business outside of possibly financial commitments would earn passive income. Sole proprietorship income is not distinguished in the data used in this analysis. Most sole proprietors, however, will be actively involved in their business (since they are sole owner) suggesting that the overwhelming majority of sole proprietor income is active.

Table 1. Distribution of Net Pass-Through Income by Business Type and AGI, 2006

Adjusted Gross Income	Sole Proprietorships	Partnerships	S Corporations
< $10k	2.12%	-11.30%	-5.84%
$10k to $20k	8.88%	0.19%	-0.08%
$20k to $30k	6.72%	0.54%	0.07%
$30k to $40k	4.84%	1.14%	0.33%
$40k to $50k	4.98%	0.74%	0.45%
$50k to $75k	10.62%	2.31%	1.94%
$75 to $100k	9.27%	2.76%	2.72%
$100k to $250k	26.65%	15.62%	13.95%
$250k to $500k	11.74%	20.45%	13.83%
$500k to $1 million	5.57%	23.72%	14.25%
> $1 million	8.60%	43.84%	58.37%
Total	100%	100%	100%
Highest Earners			
$1 million - $2 million	2.70%	16.40%	14.77%
$2 million - $5 million	4.53%	14.24%	15.95%
$5 million - $10 million	0.52%	5.64%	8.86%
> $10 million	0.86%	7.56%	18.79%
Total	8.62%	43.84%	58.37%

Source: CRS analysis of 2006 IRS Statistics of Income Public Use Files.

Figure 2 displays the distribution of active and passive income for partnerships and S corporations. As Figure 2 shows, passive income accounts for 10% of total S corporation income, and 25% of partnership income. Conversely, 90% of S corporation income and 75% of partnership income is active. A significant share of passive income from either business type is concentrated among higher income individuals (see Table A-2 in the Appendix).

WHO WOULD BEAR THE TAX BURDEN?

The analysis above found that the majority of pass-through income accrues to higher income earners.

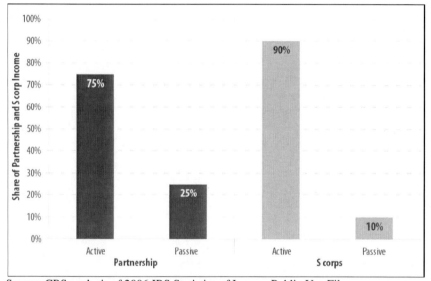

Source: CRS analysis of 2006 IRS Statistics of Income Public Use Files.
Note: The passive income measure used here does not include capital gains. The data do not allow for corporate and non corporate capital gains to be separated. Aggregate data show that capital gains are a significant income source for pass-through owners, which indicates the distributions presented could change non trivially if they could be included.

Figure 2. Distribution of Active and Passive Income by Business Type, 2006.

The income these individuals receive is the result of an ownership stake in either a sole proprietorship, partnership, or S corporation. But there are other taxpayers, namely the employees at these firms, who receive income from pass-throughs as well. If taxes are increased on passthroughs, it is possible that pass-through owners could lower wages, scale back benefits, or reduce employment in an effort to reduce the burden of the tax increase on themselves. Thus, although the majority of pass-through income is concentrated at the upper-end of the income distribution, the tax burden could be shared with lower- and middle-income taxpayers who work at these businesses.

Research on who bears the corporate tax burden can be utilized to understand who would bear the burden of increased pass-through taxation generally — owners (capital), or workers (labor).[14] The traditional analysis of the corporate tax indicates that it is capital that bears the burden. In contrast, a number of more recent theoretical studies find labor bearing the majority of the corporate tax burden. These results, however, appear to rely critically on particular assumptions (e.g., an open economy with highly mobile capital) which drive the results. When these assumptions are relaxed the burden of the corporate tax is found to fall mostly on capital, in line with the traditional analysis.[15]

There has also been a resurgent empirical interest in determining the incidence of the corporate tax. A number of recent empirical studies have found that majority of the corporate tax burden falls on labor. These studies are reviewed and critiqued in CRS Report RL34229, *Corporate Tax Reform: Issues for Congress*, by Jane G. Gravelle and Thomas L. Hungerford, who find the research is seriously flawed, produces unreasonable estimates, is not robust (sensitive to specification changes), or is inconsistent with theory. Given the unreliability of recent empirical research, and the consistency of traditional theoretical models, Gravelle and Hungerford conclude that it ""appears that most of the burden of the corporate tax falls on capital.""[16] Thus, combining the corporate tax burden research with the analysis of who earns pass-through income, it seems likely that an increased pass-through tax burden would fall mostly on higher-income taxpayers.

POLICY CONCERNS AND OPTIONS

There are several potential concerns that Congress may want to consider regarding increased taxes on pass-throughs. In some cases there may be options for alleviating these concerns. In other cases it appears that the concerns may not be validated by the data. The following discusses several circumstances that commonly elicit policy concerns.

While it appears as a general rule of thumb that higher-income business owners would bear most of the burden from increased pass-through taxation, there still may be concern about lower- and middle-income pass-through owners. For example, an across-the-board expiration of the 2001/2003 individual tax rates will increase taxes for all pass-through owners. One option for preventing the tax burden from increasing for lower and middle class business owners is to allow the reduced rates to expire only for higher-income earners. Estimates suggest a small share (3% or so) of businesses would be affected if the top individual rates were to expire.[17]

Similarly, there could be concern over the effect on lower and middle income pass-through owners from tax reform plans that call for lower corporate tax rates to be paid for by the elimination or reduction of certain "corporate" tax benefits. Scaling back corporate tax benefits, however, could raise taxes for pass-throughs since a number of corporate tax benefits are actually available to businesses more generally. An option for preventing the reduction of business tax benefits from impacting these businesses is to allow them to continue to claim the benefits. Additionally, a number of the benefits that have been considered as offsets could be reduced or eliminated without affecting smaller pass-throughs since they generally benefit corporations — including provisions related to overseas operations and fossil fuels.[18]

Lastly, there is concern that the new 3.8% unearned income Medicare contribution tax may negatively affect many small businesses.[19] As the distributional analysis showed, however, most S corporation and partnership income is the active type, and active business income is exempt from the 3.8% tax. The share of income that is passive, and potentially subject to the new tax, overwhelmingly accrues to higher income taxpayers — 77% of passive partnership income and 93% of passive S corporation income accrued to taxpayers with AGI over $250,000. Passive income earned by those with AGI of less than $200,000 (single) or $250,000 (married) would not be taxed since these taxpayers' income is not high enough to trigger the tax. Sole proprietors could generally be expected to be exempt from the tax since most of their income is likely active. It should be noted that there is one particular limitation of the data when it comes to analyzing the 3.8% tax on unearned income. The data do not allow for pass-through capital gains to be distinguished from corporate capital gains. Capital gains are considered passive income for purposes of the 3.8% tax and could be a significant income source for some pass-through owners, particularly for hedge fund managers who receive carried interest. Thus, although most ordinary pass-through income is active, pass-through owners do receive other income which is passive. Still, it is likely that if capital gains could be isolated, the distribution of capital gains would be even more concentrated among higher-income taxpayers since investment income is generally concentrated among this group. In this case, the burden of the 3.8% tax would, like pass-through taxes more generally, fall on higher-income taxpayers.

CONCLUSION

This report analyzed individual tax return data to determine who earns pass-through business income. It determined that most pass-through income is earned by higher-income individuals, although most returns reporting pass-through income are filed by lower- and middle-income individuals. The report then analyzed who would bear the burden from increased taxes on pass-through income as a result of several proposed and scheduled tax changes. Given the distribution of pass-through income, and applying research about the incidence of the corporate tax, it seems likely that in general an increase in pass-through taxes would fall mostly on higher-income taxpayers. In circumstances where there is concern that this may not be true, the report identifies options to prevent lower and middle class pass-through owners from experiencing an increase in taxes.

APPENDIX. DETAILED DISTRIBUTIONS

Table A-1. Distribution of Tax Returns and Pass-Through Income by Adjusted Gross Income, 2006

Adjusted Gross Income	Returns Reporting Pass-Through Income	% of Returns Reporting Pass-Through Income	Total Pass-Through Income	% of Total Pass-Through Income	Average Pass-Through Income
< $10k	4,478,554	16.53%	$ -26.6	-3.78%	-$5,945
$10k to $20k	3,583,598	13.23%	$ 25.6	3.63%	$7,142
$20k - $30k	2,396,688	8.85%	$ 20.3	2.89%	$8,482
$30k - $40k	2,004,143	7.40%	$ 16.5	2.34%	$8,255
$40k - $50k	1,891,013	6.98%	$ 16.6	2.36%	$8,786
$50k - $75k	3,951,384	14.59%	$ 39.2	5.57%	$9,909
$75 - $100k	2,684,429	9.91%	$ 38.0	5.39%	$14,170
$100k - $250k	4,370,055	16.13%	$137.2	19.45%	$31,398
$250k - $500k	1,026,149	3.79%	$101.5	14.48%	$98,968
$500k - $1 million	416,344	1.54%	$ 89.8	12.75%	$215,922
> $1 million	288,175	1.06%	$246.4	34.92%	$854,943
Total	27,090,675	100.0%	$704.4	100.0%	$26,011

Table A-1. (Continued)

Adjusted Gross Income	Returns Reporting Pass-Through Income	% of Returns Reporting Pass-Through Income	Total Pass-Through Income	% of Total Pass-Through Income	Average Pass-Through Income
Highest Earners					
$1 million - $2 million	167,754	0.62%	$72.1	10.22%	$429,367
$2 million - $5 million	83,776	0.31%	$76.9	10.93%	$918,840
$5 million - $10 million	22,068	0.08%	$33.6	4.77%	$1,524,106
> $10 million	14,577	0.05%	$63.8	9.06%	$4,373,348
Total	288,175	1.06%	$246.4	34.92%	$855,064

Source: CRS analysis of 2006 IRS Statistics of Income Public Use Files. Note: Averages are conditional on having pass-through income.

Table A-2. Distribution of Active and Passive Partnership and S Corporation Income by Adjusted Gross Income, 2006

	Partnership						S Corporation		
Adjusted Gross Income	Active		Passive				Active	Passive	
	% of Total	Average	% of Total	Average	% of Total	Average	% of Total	Average
< $10k	-14.46%	-$68,945	-1.93%	-$4,805	-6.45%	-$51,126	-0.19%	-$910
$10k to $20k	-0.02%	-$226	0.82%	$3,404	-0.09%	-$1,122	0.02%	$144
$20k to $30k	0.53%	$4,581	0.57%	$2,409	0.00%	$33	0.69%	$4,568
$30k to $40k	1.18%	$8,609	1.00%	$3,164	0.33%	$4,079	0.24%	$1,064
$40k to $50k	0.56%	$4,714	1.29%	$4,463	0.57%	$5,492	-0.53%	-$1,982
$50k to $75k	2.31%	$8,419	2.33%	$3,044	2.22%	$10,525	-0.49%	-$623
$75 to $100k	2.54%	$11,244	3.43%	$4,811	3.10%	$16,152	-0.63%	-$831
$100k to $250k	15.80%	$25,962	15.07%	$7,834	14.61%	$34,343	7.85%	$3,629
$250k to $500k	22.27%	$85,702	15.10%	$16,855	14.31%	$92,903	9.44%	$10,046
$500k to $1	25.33%	$164,196	18.82%	$35,986	14.26%	$203,285	13.82%	$28,982

	Partnership				S Corporation			
Adjusted Gross Income	Active		Passive			Active	Passive	
	% of Total	Average	% of Total	Average	% of Total	Average	% of Total	Average
million								
> $1 million	44.00%	$317,292	43.51%	$99,332	57.17%	$989,678	69.75%	$177,389
Total	100.00%	$42,856	100.00%	$14,833	100.00%	$63,198	100.00%	$15,344
Highest Earners								
$1 million - $2 million	17.10%	$234,605	14.39%	$60,024	14.57%	$438,348	16.81%	$73,375
$2 million - $5 million	14.43%	$335,592	13.72%	$104,740	15.53%	$939,846	19.67%	$176,540
$5 million - $10 million	5.34%	$403,422	6.54%	$168,679	8.73%	$1,844,000	10.34%	$335,604
> $10 million	7.13%	$747,393	8.86%	$310,522	18.33%	$5,628,000	22.95%	$1,041,000
Total	44.00%	$317,292	43.51%	$99,332	57.17%	$989,678	69.75%	$177,389

Source: CRS analysis of 2006 IRS Statistics of Income Public Use Files.

Note: Averages are conditional on having active or passive income from the respective business type.

End Notes

[1] This figure includes sole proprietorships, partnerships, limited liability companies (LLCs), and S corporations. The exact percentage has fluctuated over time and is sensitive to swings in the business cycle, but between 1998 (the first year pass-through income accounted for more than 50% of business income) and 2008 (the latest data year), the average fraction of income accruing to pass-throughs has been 59%. CRS calculations from Internal Revenue Service''s Integrated Business Data, Table 1, http://www.irs.gov/pub/irs-soi/80ot1all.xls. Net income is measured as net income less deficit. Regulated investment companies (RICs) and real estate investment trust (REIT) were excluded. Including RICs and REITs lowers the percentage of income accruing to pass-through over the same time period to 50%.

[2] For more information on the taxation of various business forms, see CRS Report R40748, Business Organizational Choices: Taxation and Responses to Legislative Changes, by Mark P. Keightley.

[3] For information on the role of the corporate tax and a discussion of integrating the individual and corporate tax systems, see CRS Report RL34229, Corporate Tax Reform: Issues for Congress, by Jane G. Gravelle and Thomas L. Hungerford.

[4] The data used for the analysis comes from the Internal Revenue Service''s (IRS) 2006 Public Use Tax File. This nationally representative sample of tax returns contains detailed information on individual taxpayers. There is a significant lag in the release of the Tax Files, which explains the use of data from the 2006 tax year.

[5] Nicola M. White and Drew Pierson, ""Baucus Says Congress Should Look at Taxing Passthroughs as Corporations,"" Tax Notes Today, May 5, 2011.

[6] See Senate hearing testimony by Treasury Secretary Timothy Geithner. U.S. Congress, Senate Committee on Finance, The President''s Budget for Fiscal Year 2012, 112th Cong., February 16, 2011.

[7] Martin Sullivan, ""Why Not Tax Large Passthroughs as Corporations?"" Tax Notes, June 6, 2011, pp. 1015-1018, and President''s Economic Recovery Advisory Board, The Report on Tax Reform Options: Simplification, Compliance, and Corporate Taxation, Washington, DC, August 2010, pp. 74-77, http://www.treasury.gov/resource-center/tax-policy/ Docu ments/PERAB-Tax-Reform-Report-8-2010.pdf.

[8] In the 112th Congress, Senators Wyden and Coats have introduced S. 727, which would lower corporate rate to 25% and eliminate a number of corporate tax expenditures. Ways and Means Committee Chairman Dave Camp, in a draft proposal, has pushed to lower the corporate tax rate to 25% and broaden the corporate tax base (see, http://ways andmeans. house.gov/taxreform/). The President''s National Commission on Fiscal Responsibility and Reform proposed reducing the corporate rate to between 23% and 29% and eliminating all business tax expenditures (see, http://www.fiscalcommission.gov/).

[9] For analysis on other aspects of corporate tax reform, see CRS Report RL34229, Corporate Tax Reform: Issues for Congress, by Jane G. Gravelle and Thomas L. Hungerford.

[10] For more information on the 2001/2003 tax cuts, see CRS Report R42020, The 2001 and 2003 Bush Tax Cuts and Deficit Reduction, by Thomas L. Hungerford, and CRS Report R41393, The Bush Tax Cuts and the Economy, by Thomas L. Hungerford.

[11] For more information on carried interest, see CRS Report RS22717, Taxation of Private Equity and Hedge Fund Partnerships: Characterization of Carried Interest, by Donald J. Marples.

[12] For more information, see CRS Report R41413, The 3.8% Medicare Contribution Tax on Unearned Income, Including Real Estate Transactions, by Mark P. Keightley.

[13] See, for example, Letter from Susan Eckerly, Senior Vice President, Public Policy, National Federation of Independent Business, to Senator John Cornyn, October 19, 2011, http://www.nfib.com/issues-elections/issueselections-item?cmsid=58534.

[14] See CRS Report RL34229, Corporate Tax Reform: Issues for Congress, by Jane G. Gravelle and Thomas L. Hungerford for a review and critique of recent empirical results regarding the burden of the corporate tax.

[15] The traditional view on the incidence of the corporate tax originated with the development of the ""Harberger model"" in 1962 and subsequent refinements. See Arnold Harberger, ""The Incidence of the Corporate Tax,"" The Journal of Political Economy, vol. 70 (June 1962), pp. 215-240. A review and critique of recent theoretical research, as well as a discussion of the extensions of the Harberger model can be found in Jennifer C. Gravelle, ""Corporate

Tax Incidence: Review of General Equilibrium Estimates and Analysis"" Congressional Budget Office, Working Paper 2010-03, May 2010.

¹⁶ Both the U.S. Department of Treasury and the Congressional Budget Office assume that the burden of the corporate tax generally falls on capital. See "Treasury's Panel Model for Tax Analysis," Office of Tax Analysis Technical Working Paper 3, July 2008, table 3, footnote 2, and Congressional Budget Office, Historical Effective Tax Rates: 1976 to 2006, April 2009, p. 2, http://www.cbo.gov/publications/collections/ tax/2009/summary_table_ 2006.pdf.

¹⁷ See CRS Report R41392, Small Business and the Expiration of the 2001 Tax Rate Reductions: Economic Issues, by Jane G. Gravelle.

¹⁸ See CRS Report R41743, International Corporate Tax Rate Comparisons and Policy Implications, by Jane G. Gravelle.

¹⁹ http://www.nfib.com/issues-elections/issues-elections-item?cmsid=58534.

INDEX